MARTIN O'NEILL

THE BIOGRAPHY

MARTIN O'NEILL
THE BIOGRAPHY

SIMON MOSS

JOHN BLAKE

Published by John Blake Publishing Ltd,
3 Bramber Court, 2 Bramber Road,
London W14 9PB, England

www.johnblakepublishing.co.uk

First published in hardback in 2010

ISBN: 978 1 84454 950 4

British Library Cataloguing-in-Publication Data:

A catalogue record for this book is available from the British Library.

Design by www.envydesign.co.uk

Printed in Great Britain by CPI William Clowes, Beccles, NR34 7TL

1 3 5 7 9 10 8 6 4 2

Papers used by John Blake Publishing are natural, recyclable products made from wood grown in sustainable forests. The manufacturing processes conform to the environmental regulations of the country of origin.

Every attempt has been made to contact the relevant copyright-holders, but some were unobtainable. We would be grateful if the appropriate people could contact us.

All internal photographs courtesy of Action Images.

CONTENTS

CHAPTER 1

CHOOSING
A PATH

It is well documented that Martin O'Neill's relationship with one of British football's biggest characters, Brian Clough, was fraught at best – despite great success on the pitch. While under Ol' Big Head's tutelage, O'Neill helped Nottingham Forest win an unprecedented two European Cups and captained Northern Ireland to its best-ever performance in a major tournament. Not bad for a boy who originally found sporting brilliance at Gaelic football. These days O'Neill is one of the most respected managers in British football, having earned his spurs at non-league Grantham Town with spells at Shepshed Dynamo, Wycombe Wanderers, Norwich City, Leicester City and Celtic. However, despite Bill Shankly's claim that 'football is not a matter of life and death, it's much more than that', O'Neill also proved there is more to life than just football when he quit the Old Firm giants to take care of his wife, who was suffering from cancer.

He has since made a triumphant return to the sport with Aston Villa, where, on a budget smaller than many other rivals in English football, he has begun to mould a side capable of breaking into the Premier League's infamous top four. O'Neill's journey to the top of the game, both as player and manager, has brought him into contact with some of football's biggest names.

Martin O'Neill was born into an Irish nationalist working-class family in Kilrea, around 40 miles from Belfast, on 1 March 1952. He was the fourth child of father Leo and mother Greta, who would have a further two children. According to a custom in Northern Ireland, he was named after a saint: Martin de Porres, the first black American saint – who is little known outside of South America. He enjoyed a comfortable childhood, one that allowed him to fulfil both sporting and academic excellence.

Martin's father Leo was a barber by profession and a keen Gaelic football fan. He helped establish the Gaelic Athletics Establishment in Kilrea (an organisation with whom Martin would have a major confrontation in his teens) and Leo's love of sport would quickly rub off on the young Martin. The O'Neill family lived in a council-owned house in Woodland Park. The village, while suitably distanced from unpredictable Belfast (it lies in County Derry), was not immune to the Troubles; a total of seven paramilitaries were killed in the quiet village during the unrest. However, as a trip to the area will show, both Loyalist and Unionist flags are flown.

O'Neill credits his parents, who were 'not particularly well educated' – to use his own words – with giving him wonderful values and culture. Despite his father's strong ties to the GAA, a source of great pride and tradition for many Irish Catholics, the obvious divide in Northern Ireland did not lead to isolation and segregation. In Leo's barber shop he hung a picture of the Busby Babes, Manchester United's legendary side shortly before the Munich Air crash of 1958. Most of Leo's customers were Protestants, traditionally United supporters, and Martin admitted the decision may have been motivated by business. He has always maintained that, other than the occasional border skirmish with the IRA and RUC, he never felt threatened in his childhood. At a lecture in Áras an Uachtaráin, the official residence of the President of Ireland in Dublin, he told of his father's many qualities: 'He had great common sense and I believe myself that he had a greater tolerance of things. I felt this tolerance he had shown towards the other side of the community did stand me in fantastic stead throughout the rest of my career. In this background I flourished, it was very, very strong.'

O'Neill's two older brothers were both promising sportsmen and it was no surprise that he followed suit – particularly with larger and stronger opponents to compete against at the family home. Depending on the season, the O'Neill boys would turn their garden into a football field, tennis court and even a cricket pitch. Martin was forced to raise his game to compete with his older brothers, and his brother, Leo junior, recalled the competitive streak that ran throughout the O'Neill family, telling the *Daily Record*: 'There seemed to be a competitive instinct in the family that nothing was ever treated jokingly. Everything was a competition. Nothing was worthwhile unless it was competitive. I never tried to analyse it, because that's just the way we were.'

Perhaps the most common bond between the O'Neill men, other than a love of sport, was a shared passion for Celtic Football Club. During his childhood, Celtic players such as John McPhail and Jock Weir would travel to Kilrea, as some of the club's shareholders came from the area, and would get their hair cut at Leo senior's shop. O'Neill recalled: 'The boys would frequent my father's shop and they would talk and argue about soccer. I remember them arguing about Charlie Tully. McPhail told my father that as soon as they got Tully to Celtic Park they would teach him a few things. But the following year McPhail admitted they couldn't teach Tully anything.'

O'Neill was not short of childhood heroes and idolised Ferenc Puskas, the Hungarian legend widely regarded as one of the game's true greats. Having read in a magazine about his ability to keep up a tennis ball 200 times without dropping it, O'Neill was desperate to achieve the feat. Leo junior recalled: 'I would go into the garden and would manage twenty, then Martin would come in bathed in sweat and say he had done twenty-five. This would go on into the next day. I would put the marker up to fifty...then Martin would make it up to a hundred. After a week and a half, Martin had done 200 with ease. I packed it in, but he kept it on. He was a fierce competitor from an early age, no matter what the sport would be.'

It is clear from the way Leo speaks about his younger brother that Martin, supported by a competitive family but with a strong individual will, was not a difficult youngster and rarely required discipline from his parents. Leo continued: 'Martin had established a code of conduct for himself that didn't necessitate any kind of dictate from our mother or father as to how or what way he should behave. He had programmed himself, with his ethics of living, with his ambition and what he wanted to do. He had all these attributes that he maintained and nourished, but there was a certain element of luck that you require to get on – he had a bit of that as well.'

As his brothers were accomplished sportsmen, Martin would travel to support them, something that, no doubt, spurred him on to achieve similar sporting success. In 1958, at the age of six, he made the six-hour round trip to Dublin to watch his brother in the All-Ireland final. It was the childhood equivalent of a trip to Mecca. He recalled the trip fondly during his speech at Áras an Uachtaráin: 'I loved Gaelic [football]. My older brothers ended up playing for County Derry and I spent a lot of time with my father supporting them greatly. In 1958, County Derry got to the All-Ireland final and my brother, who was eighteen, was playing. My mother decided to take me to the game. So we set off on this journey and I have never forgotten it. Within 15 or 20 miles we had picked up these two young women from Derry. They were magnificent singers and through every county we passed, each time we hit the county the girls would sing the appropriate song for that county. This journey was everything I hoped and wanted it to be. With my mother beside me I felt pretty safe. Derry lost the final.'

Despite growing up in a proud nationalist family, O'Neill only spent three years learning Irish at school, something he deeply regrets. His primary school, St Columba's Primary School at Rasharkin in Kilrea, served as a reminder of the segregation in the country, or the 'other community' as O'Neill called it: no Protestant children attended it. He passed his Eleven Plus while he was there and won a scholarship to attend St Columb's College – one of the most highly regarded establishments in Northern Ireland. Both his older brothers had attended the school, which had the distinct honour of producing two Nobel prize-winners: John Hume, the SDP MP for Derry – who played a major part in the Good Friday Agreement; and poet Seamus Heaney, who collected the prize for literature in 1995. O'Neill was at ease in school. He said: 'I was reasonably bright, reasonably academic and yet I could not seem to master Irish. Perhaps it was my schoolteacher, who used to pull on my earlobes like you wouldn't believe. So if you think I have big ears, he is responsible. There seemed to be more appealing things at the time.'

The introduction of television into mainstream society opened the eyes of many to the wider world and O'Neill was no different. It was the first time he had seen the first division of English soccer. He saw the passion of tens of thousands of fans cheering on some of the world's greatest players in a sport with a much larger following than Gaelic. As a youngster, O'Neill had proved himself a multi-talented sportsman but it was true that soccer stirred something within. He was hooked – but not just on sport. Shortly before his tenth birthday O'Neill was gripped by a high-profile trial on the mainland. In 1961, James Hanratty, a car thief, was convicted of the murder of Michael Gregsten and sentenced to death. He was the last man to be executed on British soil. From a young age, law and criminology would fascinate O'Neill and he devoured all the information on the trial he could get his hands on.

Childhood friends of O'Neill have said it was obvious he was destined to become a star. On the sports field he outshone everyone and was a natural leader. But it was at St Columb's that Martin felt his first pangs of loneliness. He had grown up in a large family in a close-knit community, and being away from his parents for the first time at boarding school was an unsettling experience. He seemed to find solace on the sports field, however, and continued to flourish as a Gaelic footballer where, following in the footsteps of older brothers Leo and Gerry, he became part of the County Derry minors side that flourished in the All-Ireland competition. Sean Moynihan, a geography teacher at the school as well as the Gaelic football team trainer, recalled: 'Martin was very skilful, with tremendous ball control and could pass with either foot. He was very difficult to dispossess once he got the ball and people had to foul him. He was not tall but was strong, stocky and had a great balance. He was a loss to Gaelic football because he was so talented.'

It was also while playing in County Derry that O'Neill first laid eyes on Geraldine McGrath, then 15 years old.

The two were introduced by a priest and resulted in the greatest, enduring love story of Martin's life.

St Columb's' pedigree helped shape Martin and allowed him to pursue a wide spectrum of interests, but at the age of sixteen, prompted by his father's need for work, the O'Neill family made the move east to Belfast. It meant Martin, who was preparing for his O-levels, had to change schools, and he took a place at St Malachy's college. While he soon earned a place on the school's Gaelic team, he also continued to play soccer and joined Rossario, one of Belfast's biggest youth clubs, situated on the Ormeau Road, after succumbing to the pressure of new friends to join a team. At St Malachy's, O'Neill's incredible talent for Gaelic found new levels, but, following his move to Belfast, football was taking up an increasing amount of his time. It was not rare for teenagers in the capital to indulge in both sports, but O'Neill's obvious ability in the two brought a problem not often encountered. 'They are two different sports but I never found that a problem,' he said. 'Because we had such a good school team spirit all of these players wanted to play together on a Sunday, so I joined them – and it was rough. We would go down to some country places and get our heads kicked in – they were more used to playing with a hurl [a short stick] down in some of those parts.'

In 1973 O'Neill was part of the Rosario's under-16 team that won the Down & Connor League and Cup double. As he continued to play football, O'Neill caught the attention of Northern Irish league side Distillery, a club founded by employees of the Royal Irish Distillery. Originally a cricket club founded in 1879, the players opted to make the switch to football so they could stay active during the winter months. Situated on the Grosvenor Road, a parting point for the Protestant and Catholic communities, Distillery was a solid club with a strong, passionate support that would give O'Neill the platform to display his talent for football to a much wider audience. It was an opportunity he couldn't resist. Distillery were also willing to grant him leave to fulfil his Gaelic commitments.

Team-mate Allan McCarrol recalled the first time O'Neill walked into the dressing room, telling the *Glasgow Daily Record*: 'He was only about eighteen and I was about thirty. The manager brought him into the dressing room and said to me: "Would you look after this wee lad?" Only he wasn't too wee; he was well built and strong. Once you saw him playing, you knew by looking at him he was going to make it.'

Despite the club's precarious position in the capital, McCarrol believes social tensions did not affect the team. 'Religion didn't matter to us,' he continued. 'Some of us were living in the Falls Road, and others in the Shankhill, but we all worked for each other – it was brilliant. We were a team who went out and played football, nothing else mattered.'

But although O'Neill's football career seemed to be on the up, political rumblings in the background about his participation in both sports would soon come to the surface. His continuing Gaelic career at St Malachy's, a college with a proud history in the sport, became a source of great friction that would leave him utterly disillusioned. The problem lay in a GAA rule that banned members from taking part in 'foreign sports'. O'Neill's commitments to Distillery did not sit well with the GAA and at the time it was big news. Rule 27 even forbade members from watching sports such as football, rugby or cricket. The rule was not always followed to the letter across all of Ireland as it would have stopped the other O'Neill men from watching Martin play. Distillery were happy to indulge O'Neill's Gaelic commitments and allowed him to miss their Irish Cup semi-final with Glenavon to represent St Malachy's in the Ulster College's GAA semi-final against St Mary's. But the GAA were not quite so accommodating in return. They were adamant the game could not take place at Casement Park in Belfast but compromised by allowing the fixture to be moved to neighbouring County Tyrone. The bitter wrangle only heightened O'Neill's reputation and the inflexibility of the GAA confused him. He told the *Irish News*: 'I found it perturbing; it left a real taste. I could not believe it. My father, who had been a major supporter of the GAA, was desperately disappointed. I think there was a culture change in him. He felt let down and I certainly did. The colleges still wanted me to play the game, to be involved and contrive to have a different venue outside Belfast, a neutral venue, where I could play the game. I did play the game and I felt it perturbing. Perhaps for a second I started to reflect on my own identity.'

O'Neill left St Malachy's with an A in Ancient History and Bs in English Literature and Latin – enough to secure him a place at Queen Mary's University in Belfast studying law. But, as O'Neill's Distillery side went from strength to strength, football would steadily take centre stage in his life. The young midfielder soon became indispensable to the club. While the club's league form was respectable, it was in knockout competitions that they really came into their own. They set up a 1971 Irish Cup semi-final with Glentoran – managed by former Aston Villa legend Peter McParland. He recalled this early encounter with the now Villa boss. 'I suppose he is the best player Distillery ever produced,' he said. 'That day Martin did as much as anybody to make sure Distillery won. You could see he was at the start of a great career. He was at university at the time, studying law, but quite a few clubs in England were trying to sign him. He was a very clever fellow but I am glad he stuck with football. We knew he did not have long before some club would take him away to England.'

Having made it through to the final, O'Neill's Distillery faced Derry City in the Irish Cup final. He netted both goals in a breathless final at Windsor Park. His second goal, fondly recalled by anyone associated with Distillery, saw him dribble past three defenders before producing a stunning strike to round off a great day for the club. Victory gave them the chance to compete on the international stage in the Cup-Winners' Cup and they were drawn against Barcelona – a giant of European football. The Catalans proved too strong for the plucky Irish, winning 3-1 at home and 4-0 away. It was O'Neill who netted Distillery's solitary goal. The club's keeper, Roy McDonald, recalled the moment fondly: 'Martin picked up a pass and went through, beating a couple of defenders before tucking the ball into the net. It was a very good goal. He had a few more chances over there. I remember he was through twice but he kicked the ground and the chances were lost. He was a deep thinker. It didn't faze him playing against Barcelona; he just went out and played his normal game. We had a great time and went over there for a week, but they really pulled the wool over our eyes. They offered to show us round the stadium and even took us to the chapel there. The place was so imposing, but it was Martin's introduction to the big time.'

Distillery's grand European adventure may have fallen at the first hurdle but a trip to the Nou Camp – a cathedral of world football – was an experience none of the squad would ever forget. It was not the last time O'Neill would travel to the Catalan capital.

Terry Neill rewarded O'Neill with his first cap for the national side and teams from England started to send scouts to assess him. Manchester United and Arsenal had been credited with an interest, but it was mid-table Nottingham Forest who would secure the signing of the nineteen-year-old for £25,000. His mother Greta wanted him to stay and finish a university degree at Queens, but Martin's mind was made up and he opted for a move to England. After years of juggling football, Gaelic and his studies, O'Neill had made his final decision and there was no going back.

CHAPTER 2

THE CLOUGH CONUNDRUM

*'Everybody thinks Brian Clough taught me all
I know in football, but that isn't strictly true.'*

Despite his mother's concerns, O'Neill signed for Matt Gillies' Nottingham Forest in 1971 – he had decided to forge a career in football. He left Queens University, Belfast, without completing his studies, and so O'Neill knew he had to step up in class and compete in England quickly if he was not going to regret his decision. Having finished second in the old First Division in 1967 and regularly attracting crowds of 40,000, Forest were on something of a downward spiral by the time O'Neill joined. Typically honest, he admits he fell into the trappings of many young footballers who have gained a dream move to England. He'd been a sought-after star in his home country, so the young O'Neill took time to understand the squad-based nature of the English game and struggled with the prospect of a place on the bench.

He told the *Daily Record*: 'I remember my early days with Nottingham Forest. Matt Gillies was the manager who brought me over. He was a very fine man and I thought, "He has bought me so he must think I am a great player." Of course, that lasted for about a week. I got into the first team quite early after coming from Irish football and – amazingly – I got left out after a game or two. I was so big headed I thought, "How can he possibly leave me out of this team?" There I was asking for a transfer within six weeks of arriving at the club. I cringe with embarrassment when I think about it now. Having an opinion of yourself isn't too bad, especially when no one around you shares that opinion, but sometimes you have to be a bit more realistic about your ability.'

Sadly, months into his Forest career, a firebomb attack razed his former club Distillery's Grosvenor Park to the ground – and with it most of the club's records. The club had to leave the site where it had spent most of its existence and were forced to ground share with a number of neighbouring clubs until 1980, when they moved to a new stadium in Ballyskeagh Road. To symbolise the clubs rise from the ashes, the club's badge was designed with a phoenix on a football.

At this stage, O'Neill, playing in a sport that could transcend social tensions, may have been immune to the Troubles taking place in his homeland, but Forest were having their own problems on the pitch. In the summer of 1972, less than a year after he joined the club, Forest were relegated to the second division and Gillies promptly tendered his resignation. His replacement, Dave Mackay, an inspiration for O'Neill, reinstalled a sense of confidence in the young Irishman who was yet to hit top form on the mainland. O'Neill recalled: 'Matt left and Dave Mackay came in. He took me under his wing and my career blossomed. When he left to go to Derby County it was a massive blow. A new manager came in, Allan Brown, and he didn't fancy me one bit. I was in and out of the team at that time, always blaming the manager and, of course, never blaming myself. Anyone who was prepared to listen would be told the manager doesn't play my style of game and that he didn't know one footballer from another. The truth of the matter was that I didn't look closely enough at myself.'

Indeed, O'Neill's own mediocrity was matched by the club as a whole, who were unable to bounce back to the top tier of English football and were found languishing in mid-table for a number of seasons.

Upheaval is catastrophic for any football club and Forest certainly lacked stability. A succession of managers at the City Ground hampered O'Neill's development in England, while he has admitted his own character contributed to this. To make matters worse, the Troubles that had plagued both Ireland and Northern Ireland suddenly spilled over onto the mainland, causing friction for the young Irishman trying to ply his trade in England's top flight. He said: 'When I went to Nottingham Forest it was the early 1970s and the political climate in England was definitely challenging. We had within months a situation where the IRA bombing was taken to the mainland and I don't think before the Troubles in Belfast really bothered the everyday

Englishman. Now, suddenly, when the bombing was taking place in London and other cities, it was on their back door and it became more frightening, it became more hostile and certainly being Irish in those days was a worrying time.'

O'Neill was acutely aware of the difficulties in being an Ulsterman seeking a career in England. As soon as the Troubles began to affect the mainland, it had a ripple effect that affected the way he was perceived among some team-mates.

High-profile attacks and the deaths of innocent people led to many uncomfortable moments for O'Neill, who admitted there were occasions when he was accused of sympathising with attackers. 'I believed that sport in general or maybe football could transcend politics, but you always felt – especially in those days of 1974 and 1975 – where there were a couple of comments made in the dressing room that suggested you would have an empathy, if not a downright collusion, in events. Irish centres were being firebombed in retaliation and I must admit it was a difficult time. Perhaps I am making too much of it, but I felt there was a kind of shadow hanging over events and it would be terrific if the situation could be resolved and resolved peacefully.'

Back on the pitch, Forest, under Alan Brown, reached the quarter-finals of the FA Cup, a considerable feat for a Second Division club, but, in early 1975, Brown too found his head on the block. On 6 January he was replaced by Brian Clough, who had won the championship with Forest's bitter rivals Derby County in 1972. At the time

Forest were in thirteenth place in Division Two. They ended the season in sixteenth.

Having delivered Derby County the first title in their history there was suddenly reason for optimism at the City Ground. Clough had an aura, a strong character and a track record of getting results. It was with this man that O'Neill would enjoy the most controversial and successful days of his playing career. Martin O'Neill and Brian Clough endured a tempestuous and well-documented relationship. O'Neill recalled he was often told by Brian Clough to sit next to him – as the Forest manager claimed it made him look better. O'Neill admitted on many occasions that his perceived arrogance brought conflict with many characters in the game – and characters didn't come any bigger than Brian Clough. Most recently, Sir Alex Ferguson has been credited with moulding a new generation of British managers from his former players: Steve Bruce, Roy Keane, Paul Ince, Mark Hughes and many more have gone on to manage in the Premier League. The same was said of Martin O'Neill who, after enjoying good times as a manager, had to put up with many people attributing his success to his former boss at Nottingham Forest.

O'Neill undoubtedly respected Clough, even if the two did not see eye to eye on many things. O'Neill was an intelligent, proud, articulate man with staunch family values and it is hard to tell why he did not get on with Clough – who shared many of the same values. But it is no secret they did not like each other.

'I have often said that it would have been difficult to

work with that man for five years and not have learned anything from him,' he told the *Irish Times*. 'You would have to be dense not to that. But I have often thought that if you tried to copy someone like Brian Clough you would find yourself in a moment of crisis to think what he would do. Even worse, you would probably be tempted to phone him for help. That is probably why I have never phoned him up in my life. If something goes wrong, at least it will be me who has made the decision, not a clone.

'I never got on with him too cleverly when I was at Forest. I used to think that I had done quite well in this game or that, and he would come into the dressing room and praise everyone else and leave me out of it. Like all of us to one extent or another, I thrived on praise and I was not getting it from him. I was always in the team when it counted, I suppose, which should have been praise enough, but he spent most of his half-time praising John Robertson or John McGovern. He didn't really have any time left for me. I would speak up, but it was always a sort of sarcastic remark. I have realised now that that is crap when you do that as a player and crap when you do that as a manager.'

He continued: 'I can remember him walking into Nottingham Forest's training ground in January 1975 to take over when the club was in the Second Division and going nowhere. Within five years, we had won the championship and two European Cups. The fact is that Nottingham Forest would never have achieved the kind of success they had without Brian Clough. I have always said – and Cloughie would say the same thing – that there can only be one of everyone, and certainly, even if I tried to, I could never have been another Brian Clough.'

Clough's first season in charge brought an immediate improvement as Forest finished eighth, albeit some way short of a promotion push. 'Cloughie liked characters,' O'Neill told the *Sunday Mail*. 'He signed a couple of important players to help young lads like John Robertson, myself, Viv Anderson and Tony Woodcock. Larry Lloyd joined from Coventry where he had caused a bit of mayhem but was a character and Cloughie dealt with him. Kenny Burns came and no one had a bigger ego than Peter Shilton, apart from maybe the manager. Brian felt they would enhance the team on the field and in the dressing room – and they did. He was strict about his discipline, though. Burns joined from Birmingham City and on a pre-season trip to Germany knocked back a couple of strong beers. Contrary to popular opinion, he was not the best drinker in the world and coughed up a little near Mrs Clough, which, as you can imagine, didn't go down too well. The manager docked Kenny a few bob and told him to behave. He did and went on to win player-of-the-year the following season.'

Clough may have enjoyed the company of big characters in his dressing room, but something about this smart, arrogant Ulsterman rubbed him up the wrong way. 'I remember saying to him if Nottingham Forest didn't match my ambition I would be off,' O'Neill told the *Mirror*. 'He told me to be off then. So I went to the reserves and he called me back about four months later and said: "Are you still here?"'

The next season, 1976/77, Forest finished third behind Wolves and Chelsea and so gained promotion back to the First Division – where many felt a club the size of Forest deserved to be – but it was not enough for Clough. To achieve what he did in the game, becoming one of football's true legends, deserved respect and O'Neill lowered his guard and admitted that he was eager for the approval of the new boss. 'He was a complex man who simplified the game in the same way all great players and managers do, he never said anything to us that we did not understand,' O'Neill told the *Daily Record*. 'We desperately wanted his approval. He was a big celebrity – he was a football genius. I brought my own experience and all the little bits I had learned from those I had worked with, but, I suppose this applies to all walks of life, it is your own character and personality that matter. You need your own style and an ability to communicate is vital. I have encountered people who were full of ideas but who could not articulate them.'

O'Neill may have mellowed with age and, with hindsight, admitted his old flaws, but he has done so with great humility. He told the *Evening Gazette*: 'Brian and I had a difference of opinion about my abilities as a footballer – I thought I was good and he said I was rubbish. Having watched the videos again, I see that he was right. Genius is a word that gets used too often, but Brian really was one. He was an impossibility. He was majestic and every other adjective under the sun. I always used to wonder where Brian got such faith from – I would have loved to have known and then I would have bottled it and sold it!'

Having made great strides as a manager, O'Neill is now well placed to see the processes that a boss must go through. He told the *Daily Record*: 'Every manager eventually develops an opinion of a player – I call it a judgment – after a while. It might not be exactly the same as the previous manager nor may it be the same as the next ones. But I have to make these assessments for myself and I don't have hard and fast rules about things like this. Players may start off very well then maybe lose a bit of form over a period of a month or two and vice versa. I know from my own experience as a player that the important thing is that you have confidence in your own ability so that whoever the manager may be you will be at the forefront of events. It can always happen like that.

'When the next manager, Brian Clough, came in he forced us all to look at ourselves and reappraise our ability. Myself, John Robertson – who was a fantastic footballer – and Tony Woodcock were drifting. We were going nowhere, but we all thought we were great. The truth is, we weren't. Brian Clough eventually – and it didn't happen overnight – made us realise that we had to work hard. He had a massive influence on all of us.

'You would have had to be really bone stupid to be with Brian Clough for five or six years and not learn something from him about the art of management. It is about the art of communication as much as anything else. He was a top-class communicator and you soon knew where you stood with him. Everything was straight, plain and simple, especially when you were being told off, which only happened to me about fifteen times a day. I learned an awful lot from Brian Clough. I also learned from other managers that I didn't have fantastic respect for, even if it was how not to do the job. You have got to be yourself and I am my normal, cantankerous self. I don't spend my life wondering how people greater than me would approach a problem. I have to approach it myself. A lot of it is gut feeling, to be honest.'

The 1977/78 season marked an incredible change in fortunes for Forest. Despite it being just their first campaign back in the top flight, Forest won the league having led it for most of the season. They were also rewarded with the League Cup, becoming the first club to win both in the same year. Peter Shilton and Kenny Burns earned national praise for their exploits, but still O'Neill remained somewhat in the shadows, competing against Archie Gemmill for a spot in Clough's midfield. 'I would expect players not to be too happy when they are out of the side,' he told the *Glasgow Evening Times*. 'No one moaned more about being left out than me. At Nottingham Forest, I knocked on Brian Clough's door for fifty-two consecutive weeks and he told me the same thing every week – that I was garbage.'

Forest had shocked plenty on their way to becoming champions of England, but they were not given a prayer when they were drawn to play defending champions Liverpool in the first round of the European Cup the following season. O'Neill did not play in either leg in the tie against Forest's fellow First Division heavyweights, but they did progress, thanks largely to the brilliance of Peter Shilton between the posts.

In the quarter-finals, Swiss club Grasshoper Zurich posed an awkward test for Clough's side, but O'Neill was able to have more of an impact in the tie, netting the equaliser in the second leg with Forest already leading 4-1 from their clash at the City Ground. The purchase of Trevor Francis, reputed to be the first player to cost £1 million – though Clough would tell you differently – was another threat to O'Neill's spot on the right side of midfield. He told the *Sunday Mail*: 'At Nottingham Forest I used to wonder who Brian Clough was going to sign and always hoped it wouldn't be someone for the right wing – then he paid one million for Trevor Francis. It gave the club and the dressing room a real lift and that is the kind of positive impact a quality signing can have.'

Despite his acceptance now that the signing of Francis was a positive thing for the club, at the time it caused heartache for the Ulsterman as Forest continued to defy the odds in Europe. O'Neill recalled the gruelling semi-final slogs against German side Cologne. He told the *Mirror*: 'I remember everything about those Forest games. In the Cologne semi-final, the state of the City Ground pitch was awful. Cologne were 2-0 up after 18 minutes. We got a goal back, but then a Belgian player missed a great chance to make it 3-1. Pre-match reports suggested they weren't quick, but they were the quickest side I had ever played against. But we settled and I thought John Robertson had given us a glorious 3-2 win when he scored with a header of all things, but then a Japanese player came on to make it 3-3. The ball had gone under Peter Shilton's body and there was terrible despair. Cologne, for all their international players, didn't know how to approach the game.'

But they did secure victory over Cologne, giving Forest a fantastic opportunity to win the grandest prize in world football. Swedish side Malmo – the same club who sold Ole Gunnar Solskjaer to Manchester United – were the opponents in a final match-up few would have predicted at the start of the campaign. O'Neill admitted his nerves were cut to shreds awaiting the announcement of the team to step out at Munich's iconic Olympic stadium. He told the *Evening Times*: 'I was stuck in a corner on the day of the game with Archie Gemmill and Frank Clarke, to be told Brian Clough could only play one of us. Clarke got it because he was eighty-six on his next birthday and might not get another chance,' he joked. 'I had been injured and did not train for three weeks before the final. Trevor Francis, who had been signed during the course of the season, was only eligible to play when we reached the final. In the euphoria of us beating Cologne in the semi-final, I am quite sure that if the final had been the following day, Brian Clough would have named the same team. Unfortunately, it was not, and in the interim Archie and myself got injured. At the end of the day, the manager went in with the side he believed could win. A week later, Northern Ireland played Denmark and I was taken off at half-time. When I got back to the City Ground, Clough said: "See, I told you you were not fit." What he didn't realise was, I was just rubbish. So, Munich to me is a place of frustration.'

O'Neill's experiences as a player – and he admitted to

deceiving managers over the course of his career – mean he is well placed to judge the players' fitness in the modern day. 'Of course there is a danger that lads who aren't fit will tell me they are,' he told the *Sunday Mail*. 'I did it when Forest made their first European Cup final against Malmo. I took a thigh knock three weeks before the big match. But, let's face it, as long as you can still walk on two legs you will tell the manager you are okay. Whether I would have started even if I had been fully fit, I don't know. Trevor Francis was eligible for the first time and would have taken his place in the team anyway. But you are a player; you want to play. Forest were in a European Cup final. Okay, if you had told me that morning I would be on the bench but the next year we would be in the final again, in the Bernebeu, against Hamburg, I would be in the team and we would win – I would have sat back, had a fag and thought the world was okay. But the chances of that happening were slim. Archie Gemmill was in the same boat as me, as was Frank Clark. We all declared ourselves fit that morning – and Clough told us we were all liars. He still played Clarky though!'

He continued: 'I think we always felt he was bonkers. He was a manic genius. There was a drop of insanity about it all, although, to be perfectly honest, there was usually method in his madness. If it got the desired result, as it invariably did with us – for a period of time we were incredibly successful – then you had to say it worked.'

Clough later talked about the moment Forest won the Cup, fondly recalling: 'When I sit in my garden and close my eyes I can still see that moment in Munich when

Robertson made his move. Peter Taylor stiffened beside me and grabbed my arm. Robertson is not far from the corner flag. There are half a dozen Malmo players in the box. Trevor Francis is hurtling towards the far post, and Robbo sends over the perfect cross. One-nil. Pass me the European Cup. Thank you.'

Despite the crushing blow of not playing in Munich, O'Neill stayed very much a part of Clough's plans. For all their gripes, Clough never once tried to get rid of the Irishman. Having played him in the reserves for match after match and, despite having him bang on his door for a game week after week, Clough continued to play the Ulsterman and it is testament to O'Neill that, when fully fit, Clough played him in the 1980 European Cup final. As he admitted, O'Neill was delighted to find himself in the starting line-up for Forest's second European Cup final – a feat that could not have occurred in most Forest fans' wildest fantasies. Ajax and Dynamo Berlin were both put to the sword in Forest's remarkable run to the showpiece event – at Real Madrid's outstanding Santiago Bernebeu stadium. O'Neill, starting in his favoured right-wing position, played an integral role as Forest retained the trophy – beating German side Hamburger SV by a goal to nil. Hamburg, who included Kevin Keegan among their ranks, were left devoid of ideas and could not overturn the one-goal deficit.

O'Neill recalled a particular moment that summarised his relationship with Clough: the brash, cocky youngster squaring off against the old master. 'We were playing Leeds at the City Ground one day,' he told the *Daily*

Record. 'The clock behind one goal was showing 3.23 – and I still hadn't touched the ball. Cloughie came in at half-time and said: "You and I are going to fall out." But I riled him by saying that everything was going down the left to John so that he could be the creative one. Then he said to me, "That's as it should be because he is the genius and you're the hod carrier."'

But after Clough's death, O'Neill paid a glowing tribute to the great man. 'He was absolutely sensational, and I don't think Brian would disagree with us either,' he told the *Express*. 'He would be the first to say that he was the greatest of all time, a bit like England's version of Ali. He had a great opinion on football, and an opinion on everything else. One of the great myths was that he was a manager and not a coach, but the truth is that every day was a coaching lesson from him. When he did come down to the training ground you would pick up enough in 25 minutes to last you a lifetime.'

O'Neill had deep respect for Clough as a family man – values that were deeply entrenched in his own life – and there was one thing the pair saw eye-to-eye on. He told the *Birmingham Post*: 'I am a great advocate of a mid-season break. It can be good but, of course, it can work the other way. I just feel it is the same squad and the same players going into every game every week. A genius used to take us away – Brian Clough. While it didn't please all of the wives, I remember it did please some of them! I remember once he sent some flowers to the wives as a sort of token and one of the players' wives told him where to put them! (. . .) As a player, I was nervous because I felt if I didn't make a good start to a match then Cloughie would take me off. In management, I get the same feeling.'

O'Neill, though not begrudging of the newfound player power in football, accepts it has changed since his day. 'In my time as a player, players had no power whatsoever. You played where you were told, the manager decided what you earned and you were lucky if you were involved with a top manager like Brian Clough as I was. Now the players are in power. But I will never begrudge the top-quality players from being paid top dollar. These are the ones who bring people into the stadia. But when the money is handed down to very average players and they have that power, that becomes an irritant,' he told the *Birmingham Evening Mail*. 'When I left Nottingham Forest after ten years, in 1981, and ended up leading a side to the quarter-final of the World Cup, do you think that Brian Clough was quaking in his boots saying: "I think he has proved me wrong"?'

CHAPTER 3

LIFE AFTER FOREST

'Unlike most non-league clubs, who are desperate
for an FA Cup run to keep the club alive, for us it is no more
than a fantastic diversion from trying to get out of the
Vauxhall Conference.'

By the time the 1980/81 season got underway O'Neill was growing frustrated at the lack of first-team opportunities and was willing to look elsewhere for regular football. Back on the pitch, Forest had the chance to become Britain's first world club champions after qualifying as champions of Europe – and they flew out for the inaugural Toyota Cup. While the competition has now begun to earn some credibility, with Manchester United sending out a full strength squad to compete following their Champions League victory in 2008, O'Neill admitted it did not have the same kudos back then. 'We didn't treat the game seriously enough,' he told *The Sunday Times*. 'It was like a glorified friendly. A holiday. I remember the rock group Queen were on our flight out to Japan and when we arrived at Tokyo airport there were hundreds of people in the terminal. We thought they might be waiting for us, but it was the like the film *10*, when Dudley Moore is dreaming about Bo Derek and they're running towards one another on the beach and, just as they seem about to embrace, she runs on by. So all the screaming fans, of course, raced past us to mob Brian May and the other members of Queen. World Cup fever hadn't quite hit Tokyo back then. When you consider now that Japan have hosted the World Cup, we actually played the game on what was basically a dirt track, not a blade of grass on the pitch. And these games had been infamous in the past because of trouble between the respective teams and supporters – which was why we were playing in Tokyo, the first time one of these games was held on a neutral ground. It was a mundane match, generally free of incident. We should have beaten them, and that's the disappointment. We had a couple of great chances. I remember the doctor advising us to stick as best we could to British time in terms of our sleeping patterns, as we had to play a match the following Saturday; there was no such thing as switching domestic fixtures to Sundays in those days. The game just wasn't taken seriously. The following year Liverpool were beaten 3-0 by Flamengo and they said the same as us. They treated it like a glorified friendly. We really should have won it.'

Frustrated by the wide role in which he was continually asked to play by Clough, and craving a more central position where he could have more influence on the game, O'Neill moved to Norwich City in February 1981.

Despite having left his studies behind in Belfast, O'Neill

maintained an active interest in law alongside the rigours of playing for Norwich City – a club with big ambitions of its own. In 1981, Peter Sutcliffe, the Yorkshire Ripper, went on trial and O'Neill was fascinated, just as he had been by the Hanratty case in his youth. At the trial Sutcliffe pleaded not guilty to thirteen counts of murder but guilty to manslaughter on the grounds of diminished responsibility – claiming he was carrying out God's will. O'Neill made sure he got a seat at the trial. He recalled in the *Daily Mirror*: 'For the Ripper trial I queued overnight with my heavily pregnant wife. We lined up for the 9am start until the afternoon session and we were the last two let in. There must have been 200 other people behind us in the queue.'

However, the Ripper trial would prove a rare highlight in the year for O'Neill, who would leave East Anglia after only eleven appearances – and the one goal – as a massive offer from the North West proved irresistible for both club and player. Manchester City paid £250,000 to bring the midfielder to Maine Road in June 1981.

By his own admission, O'Neill was 'crap' during his spell at Manchester. He told the *Scotsman*: 'John Bond bought me and could not wait to get rid of me.' He returned to Norwich for half that fee in February 1982 after just thirteen first-team appearances for the Maine Road outfit. His eventual return to Norwich was certainly more successful as he bagged eleven goals in fifty-five appearances between 1982 and 1983. A move to Notts County in 1983 would give O'Neill, now in his mid-thirties, a chance to play first-team football at a high standard, but his goal-scoring ratio diminished as the years passed. In the desperate hope of proving his fitness for the 1986 World Cup, which Northern Ireland had again qualified for under Billy Bingham, a knee injury finally ruled him out of a trip to Mexico – and indeed his whole playing career.

In the twilight of their careers, footballers find themselves at a crossroads in their lives. While many do indeed go down the route of management, cutting their teeth in the lower leagues before hopefully moving up the leagues, it is certainly not for everyone.

With O'Neill, an intelligent man with options outside of the game, the choice was not an obvious one. Despite this, he again sided with continuing his football career and in the end was left frustrated by a number of non-league clubs who refused to speak to him. The first club that did was Grantham Town, then playing in the Beazer Homes League, Midlands Division. Grantham, in Lincolnshire, the town that gave the world Margaret Thatcher, was used to famous former players gracing the club, but having a former European champion at the helm was still considered a serious coup. After signing in the summer of 1987, O'Neill had to fulfil contractual obligations to coach across the Atlantic in the USA before taking charge. As a result, pre-season training was carried out by former Nottingham Forest team-mate John Robertson. It was touch-and-go as to whether O'Neill would even make it to the club's first league game, against Welsh side Merthyr Tydfil, in time. Despite having spent weeks on a different continent, O'Neill in a show of commitment to his new club, went straight to the match from the airport. However, even though the arrival of a new manager would eventually buoy the club, the transformation was far from immediate: Grantham slumped to a 3-0 defeat in O'Neill's opening game in charge.

However, despite the inauspicious start, Grantham rapidly improved and found themselves at the summit during the festive period. Certainly having the charismatic Martin O'Neill as boss was rubbing off on his charges as they began to play the style of football their new gaffer demanded. The squad responded to his methods, training and ideas of how he wanted the game played. He had assembled a group of players with both youth and experience who were playing a brand of football he felt acceptable. When O'Neill arrived at the club, getting more than 200 people at the gates was considered a result at Grantham Town; by the end of the season, crowds were regularly topping 1,000. Despite the gathering momentum, however, Grantham missed out on promotion by a single point.

Considering the drastic improvement made by his side over the season, and the disappointment of missing out on promotion, surely things could only get better the next season? But a solid campaign that saw Grantham finish fifth did little to satisfy either O'Neill or the club, both of whom were frustrated at the lack of progress. It soon became apparent that O'Neill's future might not lie with Grantham. His head was turned by ambitious plans to revolutionise the club brought forward by the management at Shepshed Dynamo. Disillusioned after failing to gain any more assurances about funds coming into the club, and sensing the project at Shepshed represented a new career challenge, O'Neill abandoned Grantham – the first club to give him a chance at management – and became Shepshed manager in July 1989. By October, however, less than four months after taking charge, he departed: while his record on the pitch was, on the whole, fair, a series of differences of opinion with the club's upper echelons proved irreconcilable.

Many managers in the modern game get by on the strength of the name they made as a player. It is becoming increasingly common for retired players to jump straight into Championship or League One clubs without bothering to learn their new trade at a non-league club – as O'Neill did. Still, his venture into football's lower echelons could not be regarded as a resounding success – after all, he had failed to fulfil ambitious plans at either Shepshed or Grantham – but, luckily for the Ulsterman, a big club was just around the corner. Opportunities outside football once again tempted O'Neill, but the lure of the beautiful game prevailed. O'Neill took the managerial reins at Wycombe Wanderers, playing in the GM Vauxhall Conference, in February 1990, having being turned down for the role while he was still at Shepshed. A chance meeting with football commentator Alan Parry, a director at Wycombe, brought about a swift return to management with a club capable of climbing straight into the Football League.

Martin O'Neill was at the helm of Wycombe Wanderers, now a solid football league club, from 1990 to 1995. Under his stewardship, attendances at Adams Park more than doubled as he brought an exciting brand of football to the leafy commuter town. When he joined, the club was stuck in the conference and had appointed the young manager in the hope that he could secure swift promotion. He led the club to a fifth-place finish in his first season in charge, but enjoyed more success in the cup competitions, leading Wycombe to the FA Trophy final – which they won to earn O'Neill his first piece of managerial silverware.

Following their displays during his first season, O'Neill's Wycombe were touted as favourites for promotion, something that left the Ulsterman baffled. 'I think that was absolutely crazy,' he told the *Independent*. 'I don't believe the bookies know the GMVC very well.' At the end of another gruelling season, Wycombe finished runners-up in a heart-breaking climax to the race for the Football League.

At the start of the 1992/93 season Wycombe were once again among the favourites to top the Conference and O'Neill was able to retain the majority of his squad for another long, hard push. But O'Neill was still angered by the circumstances that denied Wycombe what he perceived a deserved place in the game's upper echelons. He told the *Guardian*: 'Last season we were just pipped by Colchester for a place in the Football League, but we had finished twenty-one points clear of third place, Maidstone were in financial trouble and we had sound claims for promotion. The pyramid leagues were held up for a month until a decision was made. It was almost pathetic for Maidstone to be allowed back into the league when there was no chance that they would survive the season. We have the same squad as last season and psychologically they have put last season's disappointments behind behind superbly. No one is about to bankrupt this club for five minutes of fame.'

Indeed O'Neill's determination to make Wycombe a success made him sure his club were different from others in the division. 'Unlike most non-league clubs, who are desperate for an FA Cup run to keep the club alive, for us it is no more than a fantastic diversion from trying to get out of the Vauxhall Conference,' he told *The Times*. 'We welcome the exposure and the boys will take ephemeral glory if they can. If we reach the fifth round or quarter-finals and lose out on the Vauxhall Conference, I am afraid I would commit suicide.'

O'Neill's drive and ambition could be conceived as arrogance, but he made no secret of the fact that his future would, hopefully, lie away from Wycombe. 'I want to be up there with the Dalglishes and the Sounesses,' he added. 'I played against them and I would like to be up there managing a big team. In a couple of seasons I hope I will be and I know I would relish it. It is not sounding big-headed, I hope.'

By early summer in 1993 Wycombe were all but assured of a place in the Football League and O'Neill suddenly found himself the subject of admiring gazes from clubs up and down the country. His side had won the Conference at a canter playing attractive football. Nottingham Forest, who had suffered different fortunes and were relegated, looked at their former midfielder to take the club back to the top flight. In what he agreed was a gamble, O'Neill opted against a move and signed a new contract at Adams Park. 'I am quite sure when I am managing Maidenhead two years down the line I will know I have made the wrong decision,' he joked. 'It didn't become available for eighteen years in the first place. It may be another eighteen years before it is available again – and I will be dead and buried by then. However, I have started a job at Wycombe that I would love to finish. I have a great affection for Forest, especially the fans, but I honestly could not leave Wycombe at such an important and exciting time. I genuinely would love to see Forest go right back to the top and I have this silly little dream that we could join them.' In the same season, Wycombe picked up their second FA Trophy under O'Neill in what had been a terrific double-winning season for the Adams Park club.

Throughout his managerial career, O'Neill has not been afraid to blood young players and such was the case at Wycombe. Fiercely proud of his players and, having gained confidence in the club's youth players, the Ulsterman was more than happy to give them their first starts. In their first season in the old Division Three, with the club more than holding its own, O'Neill gave an insight into how he rewarded sacrifice in young footballers. He told the *Daily Mail*: 'I feel what has happened here this season is commendable and the efforts of the players have to be appreciated. I really mean that because four or five of the young lads decided that professional footballers were what they wanted to be, even though as part-timers and with a wage from a job, they could earn more than they would as pros. I don't know whether it was the proper managerial thing to do but I decided to give them the first crack in the side this season. Because they were prepared to make such sacrifices, I was prepared to back them and see if they were good enough. I have to say the players this season have been magnificent.'

His success at Wycombe had not gone unnoticed and questions about his future would keep arising. But, as he proved with Wycombe, Celtic and Leicester, he is more than happy to stay at a club he feels is progressing. He added: 'People might think I am in a comfort zone here. But I remember something someone said to me at a golfing do in Ireland this summer when the discussion got round to whether I should take the Forest job or not. Some geezer said to me: "I'll tell you what life's about, it's about building your own business". I suppose I listened to the point and I knew I was getting a lot of satisfaction from being in at something at the beginning. I don't know how far Wycombe can go – we might have come as far as we can, but things are still happening.'

Many Conference clubs struggle to make the step up in class to the Football League and find themselves languishing in mid-table or worse. However, O'Neill's Wycombe flourished, finishing fourth in Division Three and making it through to the play-off final with a breathtaking 4-2 win over Preston North End. 'Everything we have tried to do at the club has come right today,' O'Neill proudly asserted as he plotted another successful trip down the M40 to Wembley. Not content with just a place in the play-off final, O'Neill's Wycombe completed impressive back-to-back promotions to take them to Division Two.

Having taken the club to Wembley in his first season in charge, winning the Conference in 1993 via another victory in the FA Trophy, followed by promotion from the old Division Three, O'Neill's five years in charge at Wycombe could be classed as a resounding success. However, there was the feeling that he had taken the club as far as it could go. Both O'Neill and the club had taken much from the last five years; the club was now well and truly embedded in the Football League, while O'Neill's stock as a manager had never been higher.

CHAPTER 4

CAPTAIN FANTASTIC–
THE INTERNATIONAL
YEARS

*'I feel as Irish as the day I left and I feel proud as the
day I left and that will never change and yet the irony is that I
could not have done the job I did for quite a number of years
in Ireland. I had to go and earn my living in England.'*

Martin O'Neill played sixty-four international matches for his country between 1971 and 1984 and captained the side for a spell in the 1980s, including the famous World Cup campaign in Spain in 1982. Along the way, Billy Bingham's side despatched the host nation before losing to France in the quarter-finals. It is widely regarded that, given the vastly shallower talent pool Bingam had to dip into, this feat eclipsed the Republic's similar achievement at USA '94.

At the start of O'Neill's international career, political unrest was rife in Northern Ireland, but Billy Bingham's team, especially on the field, was able to look past the great divide in the country to gain success. O'Neill was never criticised for his religion, which he attributes to the success of the team on the field, something that can transcend most barriers in society. After the turn of the century, O'Neill's then Celtic midfielder Neil Lennon was singled out for sectarian abuse due to his decision to sign for the Bhoys, but O'Neill said he was never the victim during his days playing for the national side. 'I only got booed because I was crap,' he told the *Daily Star*. 'I went to the friendly with Spain before the World Cup and went on to the field to take part in an anti-sectarian display.'

He continued in the *People*: 'It was a mixed group then, just as it is now, but probably because we were doing well everyone seemed to have something else to shout about. We were used to getting 30,000 crowds for matches at Windsor Park and it was said that maybe the team galvanised everyone in Northern Ireland at the time.'

He told the *Glasgow Herald*: 'I played during troubled times when Northern Ireland wouldn't even play at home for a number of years but, when we returned to Windsor Park, the side was evolving into a decent one. When we had a good international side...going to play for Northern Ireland was something we all looked forward to. Because we had a reasonably decent side, which qualified for a couple of World Cups, maybe everything else got squashed into the background.'

Nine years earlier, O'Neill had been part of the Shamrock Rovers XI that took on the reigning world champions Brazil and narrowly lost a fascinating match 4-3. It was the first time an all-Ireland team had competed since the split in 1921 and a lack of support from the Irish FA meant the players had to go under the banner of Rovers. The match was intended to be a gesture of goodwill at a time when the Troubles were at their most violent. Derek Dougan, the Northern Ireland striker, never played for his nation again after the fixture. O'Neill recalled: 'Derek sacrificed a lot. He knew what he was taking on – with the game being played against the particular political and religious backdrop of the time – and his own Northern Ireland career suffered as a consequence. Even then we realised that it was very historic, but you would never have known at that stage what the future held. Derek didn't reappear for Northern Ireland. He was getting on a bit in years, but he was still capable of playing international football.'

The game may not have been given much backing by the Irish FA, but the players relished the opportunity to go out and test themselves against Brazil. O'Neill insisted that for the players the political situation came second to football. He mused on whether a similar venture would be forthcoming in the modern day. 'Certainly the political climate has changed a great deal since then and I suppose you might think that, in this particular climate, it is a possibility. But I really don't know, even at this stage, if everyone wants it to happen. If everybody wants it to happen, why couldn't it? The players' view would generally be like that. I mean, George Best always cried out for a united Ireland. I know we played as Rovers because we couldn't do it any other way, but it would be a phenomenal step.' He told *The Sun*: 'Northern Ireland went to the 1982 World Cup and we played in the quarter-finals. Can you imagine what our side would have been like then if it had included Frank Stapleton and Liam

Brady? We would have been phenomenal. We had a great spirit among ourselves at that time but you can imagine what it would have been like to add one or two of those players. And I am sure there was a stage in later years when the Republic might have thought they could have done with one or two extra players – like if Pat Jennings had been around.

O'Neill was made the first Roman Catholic captain of Northern Ireland and successfully guided the club to the World Cup finals in Spain. Billy Bingham, a proud Irishman who would not let politics or social unrest affect his squad, or decisions, told the *Sunday Telegraph*: 'When I picked Martin to be my captain, I had letters. There were threats from people who didn't want him to do it. They came from bigots, cranks and idiots, call them what you want. I knew that if I was going to have a team, it had to come from all communities. I said when I took over, it will have to be from both persuasions. And it was an absolutely mixed team and I never had an ounce of trouble. They all sang each other's songs, we rejoiced together and we commiserated with each other when we lost. The team could not have done what it had if I had eleven Protestants in it or if it had eleven Catholics. Martin was a wonderful captain for us. He wanted the responsibility and he was such a bright fellow I knew he was the man for the job. And he played alongside Sammy McIlroy in the centre of midfield, a Protestant. Elsewhere in the team you had Gerry Armstrong, from the Falls Road, and Norman Whiteside, from the Shankhill. It didn't matter to us.'

Buoyed by a sense of community and togetherness

fuelled by the social unrest occurring in their own country, Northern Ireland performed brilliantly in the early stages of the '82 World Cup. They finished top of a group that included the hosts Spain, Yugoslavia and Honduras, with four points from their three fixtures. A battling goalless draw with Yugoslavia was followed up with a surprising 1-1 stalemate with Honduras, with Gerry Armstrong netting after ten minutes. The final group game against Spain would be make or break for the Irish if they wanted to continue their World Cup adventure. And, sensationally, they stunned the hosts with a 1-0 victory, Armstrong again among the goal scorers.

In the second round, under a different format to the present World Cup finals, O'Neill's Northern Ireland were drawn in a three-team group with Austria and France. Considering they had already beaten a talented host nation, there was little fear factor in the players' minds. A 2-2 draw with Austria left Bingham's team needing a result against France to make it through to the semi-finals.

Northern Ireland would meet France on a baking day in the Spanish capital. But O'Neill was denied goal-scoring glory on the biggest stage of all when he had a perfectly valid goal disallowed. 'Television replays proved I was a yard onside,' he told the *Irish Times*. 'Then a couple of minutes later, Giresse scores and they win 4-1. But if my goal had stood, I think we had a chance. It still rankles with me greatly; not being in the record books as scoring in the World Cup is soul destroying.'

The Northern Ireland squad still came home from Spain as heroes – the golden generation for a small nation bereft of any real achievement in international football. As captain, O'Neill had helped form a cohesive unit that transcended the divisions in Northern Irish society. Unfortunately for both O'Neill and his country, that was as good as it got during his playing days, and as injuries blighted the end of his career, O'Neill was unable to take part in the next World Cup, held in Mexico in 1986, and he never played for his country again.

CHAPTER 5

THE LEICESTER CITY PROJECT

'It is really nice and pleasing when people say it is a big achievement to have done what I have at Leicester, but I don't believe a word of it. Every manager in the country will eventually be judged by what they win.'

It was a huge wrench to leave Wycombe. In his five years in charge he had moulded a side that played the way he wanted – and had enjoyed great success as a result. But, the opportunity arose to take over at Carrow Road, with Norwich City keen to take on the Ulsterman. While his playing career in East Anglia had lacked spark, his spell as manager was certainly an interesting one.

O'Neill's short stint at the helm of Norwich City highlighted both a stubborn nature and an unwillingness to move from his principles. City had not made a bad start by any means under their new boss, but O'Neill's desire to bring in new blood was not shared by chairman Robert Chase. Hoping to sign Hull striker Dean Windass for around £750,000, O'Neill was left frustrated as the transfer collapsed. An exodus of players the previous season had seen the Norwich coffers swelled, yet his attempts to bring in new players were not backed up by the board. O'Neill had kept his frustrations in check but, following a 3-2 defeat to Huddersfield in October 1995 (just months after taking over), he eventually spoke out. 'I have made no secret of my view that the team needs strengthening,' he told the *Daily Mail*. 'At the moment, I have not got a clue if the funds are going to be forthcoming or not.'

The media were calling it a 'revolt' and certainly O'Neill was getting annoyed at the lack of support he was receiving from the board. It was to lead to his eventual departure. Indeed such was the strength of feeling in East Anglia that chairman Chase was advised to have a police escort to games, as disgruntled fans vented their frustrations following relegation to the First Division earlier in the year. O'Neill echoed their sentiments: 'It is time for some straight answers,' he said. 'The chairman has promised to provide those answers this weekend and I am waiting with great interest. In view of what I was told when I came here it has been very frustrating, to say the least.'

Just a month after pleading for some straight answers, O'Neill left the Carrow Road hotseat. He tendered his resignation, initially refused by Chase, ahead of a game with, ironically, Leicester. Before the match Norwich issued a statement saying: 'We regret to announce that team manager Martin O'Neill has tendered his resignation which is not being accepted. His contract still has eighteen months to run.'

Despite the board's best efforts, O'Neill's next move was

already in motion and he was installed as the new boss of Leicester City almost immediately. Within a year, Chase would resign as chairman at Carrow Road. Looking back on the whole affair, O'Neill accepted he simply could not work with the man. He told the *Guardian*: 'Working with Mr Chase was an experience. I felt I was better at managing the club than he was, but he didn't seem to share that view. If he had let me get on with the job I would probably have still been there now. I know in the mid-eighties he rescued the club, they should be grateful for that, but if he had told me from day one that there was no money to buy players, and indeed the club was broke, I would still have taken the job and sorted things out. I was not looking for £10 million to spend. It was once suggested to me that he didn't really want a manager at all, he just wanted a tracksuit. Someone had to let go and it was not going to be him. So it had to be me.'

Norwich were in the quarter-finals of the League Cup and third in the First Division when O'Neill left and he was sure he could have taken them up. But his relationship with Chase had completely broken down and it got to the stage where he could not stand it any longer. At Wycombe he had enjoyed the support of both fans and the board, but at Norwich this was not the case. The fans' support was not enough to make him stay. O'Neill maintains he had an affinity to Norwich and left with deep regrets. But Leicester had been admiring O'Neill for a while and it was an easy decision to take over at Filbert Street.

O'Neill's predecessor as Leicester boss, Scotsman Mark

McGhee, still had many supporters in the Leicester changing room and O'Neill was aware he would have to win over the squad. 'Quite a few of the players were not happy,' he recalled. 'They seemed to think that he [McGhee] would be back for them and they would follow him to Wolves. There was a lot of disillusionment because many of the players got on so well with McGhee. They didn't want to be at the club.' One such player was Steve Corica, who O'Neill allowed to leave and reunite with McGhee at Wolves. O'Neill admitted Corica had caused hassle and, as he had Muzzy Izzet and Neil Lennon on his radar, the midfielder was soon on his way out of Filbert Street.

O'Neill believed being an ex-Forest player did not endear him to the Foxes faithful at first and this was exacerbated by his failure to win any of his first ten games, including five draws and five defeats. Had this gone on another month, he felt he might have been shown the door himself. 'If you win football games, though, crowds tend to forgive you,' he concluded.

But it did not take long for O'Neill's infectious character to take hold of the squad and they rapidly improved. Former City physio Mick Yemoan explained: 'I don't know what he had, but whatever it was, he made you want to run through walls for him. I was just the physio, but by the time he had finished I could have gone out there and played. He made you feel like a king.'

In his opening season at Leicester, O'Neill was eventually able to guide the club back to the Premier League at the first time of asking, no mean feat for a new manager. By March 1996, however, in O'Neill's thirteenth week in the job, things were less than perfect at Filbert Street. Following a 2-0 defeat at home to Sheffield United, around 200 seats were torn from the South Stand as supporters called for the head of their manager. Never one to hide from his problems, and always open and honest, O'Neill spoke to a delegation of fifteen supporters after the game. He said: 'I am not going to hide away from the supporters. I am not the first manager to take stick from the fans, and I won't be the last. I am determined to get it right.'

He continued in *The Times*: 'You can either cave in or get stronger and I decided to take the latter option. People said that game was a watershed. After thirteen weeks in the job, the last thing I wanted was a watershed. The fact is that there had been a lot of false promises here. The previous manager Mark McGhee had upped and left saying the side was good enough to win the league at a stretch. That was ludicrous, because there was no appreciable difference between the top eight or nine sides. But I was landed with that prediction.'

He recalled in the *Leicester Mercury*: 'I was aware that the crowd were unhappy, but afterwards I heard that there was a protest outside and some members of the board had allowed a cross-section of fans into the club and they were discussing things. I didn't know about this, but if there was any talking to be done, I wanted to have my say. And I had my say and I hope they listened. It was a frank discussion: I said I had only been there for three months; that I needed some time; that things were not quite as rosy as they might have seemed here. I said it might not happen this season, but it would happen – Leicester City would be in the Premiership. And then we went on a little run.'

It seemed O'Neill had a nasty habit of moving to a club whose supporters were less than thrilled with the chairman. Having escaped Robert Chase, Leciester supremo Martin George was hardly revered in the East Midlands. Still, on the pitch, what a difference a month makes. By late April, Leicester were back in contention for a play-off place. O'Neill admitted it had been a turbulent twelve months. 'It has been a traumatic year for me, to say the least,' he told the *Independent*. 'Character building, I think, is the expression people use. But with Ipswich losing, we have a fighting chance of making the play-offs and I think it is deserved. I am thrilled to bits.'

O'Neill, as well as the supporters, was acutely aware that there were problems at boardroom level. 'There was boardroom friction, I could see that pretty early,' he told the *Leicester Mercury*. 'And that would make itself apparent later – but on the field, the results had not been that great either.'

Leicester were on a great run in the First Division and secured a place in the play-offs – just a few wins away from a place in the Premier League. The Foxes were pitted against Stoke City in the semi-finals, who they duly saw off in a close-fought contest. Now Crystal Palace stood between Martin O'Neill's Leicester and a place in the Premier League. O'Neill was adamant his side had what it took to go all the way. Ahead of the capital showdown, O'Neill told the *Independent*: 'I always believed enough in my own ability to know that I could succeed with Leicester, given a wee bit of time. Had we been serving up this kind of football a year into my reign I would have left without being asked. But I had only been in the job thirteen weeks or so. There was a feeling of abandonment among the team; so much so that I feel anyone taking over would have felt a backlash from the players and supporters. I told the chairman this might happen and it did. And at the same time within a couple of games I was having to make the kind of assessments of my players that you would normally make over many weeks. Jimmy Nicholl at Millwall said he wished he had done things his own way from the start, and not given everybody a chance. But I did give almost everybody a chance. At some stages I loved every minute of my time there. If I regret anything it is that in leaving Norwich maybe I let down the supporters who I felt were championing their cause against the chairman.'

The match at Wembley was far from a classic, but a last-gasp goal from Steve Claridge was enough to secure a 2-1 win for the Foxes in extra-time. O'Neill said: 'I was dreading it was going to penalties, this has to be one of the best moments of my life.'

O'Neill also joked he would have committed suicide had the team lost, but fortunately Claridge was on hand to avert any disaster. 'They were big favourites, make no mistake,' he told the *Leicester Mercury*. 'But we were in form, we were coming in off the back of a great run and confidence was high. I remember that day vividly – 40,000 people in blue and white, a tremendous atmosphere. We went a goal behind, but we never gave in. We got back into it and we deserved it, you know. Steve Walford, who was the coach at City, still says that of all the great times we had at Leicester that was the greatest. It was a fantastic day and, you know what, I wouldn't necessarily disagree with him. It was the start of it all.'

The problem for all successful Championship clubs is having your key players poached by established Premier League clubs, and O'Neill was determined this fate would not befall Leicester. He added in *The Times*: 'For years, Leicester have been a selling club. Well, I want to change that image. The way to keep players like Emile Heskey and Neil Lennon is to show them you have ambition. When they see progress is being made and they win matches, they are happy. Our problem will come if we lose key people, because I do not have the money to replace them with somebody capable of doing as good a job.'

O'Neill's first game as a manager in English football's top flight was against Sunderland in August 1996. The game, far from a classic, petered out into a goalless draw, but a clean sheet, vital in the Premier League, was enough to please the Leicester boss away from home. In the old First Division O'Neill's aggressive, powerful forward Emile Heskey had begun to make a name for himself. Like so many top goalscorers, making the step up in class to the Premier League either makes or breaks you. Fortunately for O'Neill, Heskey continued where he left off. Leicester picked up their first win of the season just days later, with Heskey hitting a double to see off Southampton at Filbert Street. O'Neill hailed his striker as 'out of this world'.

Later in August, John Robertson joined O'Neill at Leicester as assistant manager, fulfilling a role he had held at Wycombe and Norwich respectively.

'I look back on the players I signed there and I have to tell you I am pleased with that,' O'Neill told the *Leicester Mercury*. 'I think Gunnlaugssen and Fenton were the two disappointments. But I didn't, and still don't, buy a player thinking about the ratio, how many worked, how many didn't. I buy them because I think they can do a specific job.' Speaking of the step up in class in the Premier League, he continued: 'We played Liverpool at home, sixth game of the season and they beat us 3-0, it could have been 10-0. It was a real wake-up call. But the players never gave up. There was a great work ethic, a terrific attitude. You can work on that but it's an elusive quality, you can't just invent it. I remember Savage, Lennon, Izzet in midfield with Stevie Guppy up and down the left flank. There was Walsh, Elliot and Taggart at the back. It was a solid line-up, difficult to beat, but creative, too. I loved Filbert Street. I see the Walkers Stadium today and it's a fine stadium and I say well done to you, but if you could have kept Filbert Street and built up those two stands to match the Main Stand – which was superb but looked incongruous by itself – what a ground that would have been.'

The chance to pit his wits against the best clubs, players and managers is what O'Neill had waited for all of his managerial career, and the visit of Arsenal to Filbert Street represented a truly huge challenge for the Foxes. Arsenal came away with a 2-0 win at the start of a bad run of results for Leicester. Defeats to Sheffield Wednesday and

Liverpool followed as the season moved into September, but a stunning victory at White Hart Lane saw Leicester return to form in emphatic style. Steve Claridge and Ian Marshall netted either side of a Clive Wilson penalty to end a great trip south for O'Neill's side.

By Christmas Leicester had picked up wins over Leeds, Newcastle and Aston Villa as the established order in the Premier League began to sit up and take notice of the challenge from Filbert Street. Not only was their league form impressive, but Martin O'Neill was also forging a reputation as a manager who knew how to win cup-ties. Survival is always at the forefront of a newly promoted team, who invariably have smaller squads compared to their illustrious rivals, but O'Neill was still able to negotiate his way through to the last eight of the Coca-Cola Cup, knocking out Manchester United on the way. Speaking after that sensational result, O'Neill told the *Mirror*: 'Obviously Alex has his eye fixed firmly on Europe, but I hope that won't take any credit away from us. The most important thing for Leicester City is that we have beaten Manchester United to go through to the last eight of the Coca-Cola Cup for the first time in over twenty years.'

Going into the festive period having notched up an impressive twenty points, O'Neill was confident his side could stave off relegation. He told the *Mirror*: 'The last time City were in the Premiership they had picked up only fourteen points by Boxing Day. I think forty points this season might be good enough to keep us up. These games give us the chance to go into the New Year in a relatively safe position.'

Certainly Leicester's squad was not the biggest, which made survival in the brutal Premier League all the more difficult, let alone fighting on two fronts, with the League Cup dream very much alive. A whole host of injuries and suspensions in late January stripped Leicester to the bare bones, but O'Neill was not about to start making excuses. 'I have to believe that it is a situation you very rarely encounter,' he told the *Independent*. 'At Premiership level you should hardly ever get four players suspended at the same time, and all these injuries, but if you are a Premiership club you have to cope with that. We have got the smallest squad in the Premiership and the situation has exposed us.'

By February, Leicester were out of the FA Cup, courtesy of a dubious penalty decision that gave Chelsea a 1-0 win in their fifth-round replay. However, in football there are always chances to atone and O'Neill's side soon had reason to celebrate in the League Cup. The semi-final first leg against Wimbledon at Filbert Street had failed to bring a goal, meaning Leicester would have to score in the return fixture to stand a chance of going to Wembley. A 1-1 draw after extra-time may not have represented a resounding victory, but it was enough to send Leicester to the capital. O'Neill's cup magic had once again rubbed off on his squad. O'Neill, eloquent, passionate and undoubtedly successful, was earning praise from across the football fraternity. He said after the game: 'It was a long time after the goal. The game felt like 120 years in Alcatraz rather than 120 minutes. I feel like I am ninety-three. There is great character in this team, some decent players and real camaraderie. They battled away.'

Almost immediately, given the giant strides that the team had made and now they were looking increasingly secure in their top-flight status, O'Neill and Leicester opened contract negotiations. In March, Leicester were occupying ninth place, way beyond the expectations of many. Leicester chairman Tom Smeaton commented in the *Belfast Newsletter*: 'There are definite plans to make extensions to his contract. It is fair to say that we have been talking for some time. We see him as a long-term part of the club, but I am not putting a date on things in terms of when matters might be sorted out as that would be putting too much pressure on him and me. But I am sure he will be regarded even more highly in the game after what has happened this season and in helping us to reach Wembley. It is tremendous what has happened and Martin has been a revelation. He has helped put wonderful spirit into the team and everyone is so committed, but he has also brought in some fine players to go with the ones already here. However, I would not say we were surprised how things have gone or that they have exceeded expectations. I think the expectations here of myself and Martin are very high. We were asked at the start of the season, when everyone was saying we were going back down, what our ambitions were and I said ninth and Martin said to be playing in Europe. I might be a little surprised at the speed at which we are proceeding but not surprised that we are moving along those lines.'

O'Neill was finally beginning to command the respect of a

football club chairman and, with a clear path in front of him, both the Ulsterman and Leicester would flourish. Despite the assurances, O'Neill was eager to see progression at the club and would have been delighted when Leicester announced a £40 million stock market flotation to bring a welcome cash injection into the club. 'Expectation has been raised by what we have done this season and supporters will expect us to carry on from this point,' he said at the time.

Leicester would face Bryan Robson's Middlesbrough in the Coca-Cola Cup final showpiece on 6 April 1997 at a packed Wembley. Boro had invested heavily in star names hoping to bring instant success. Fabrizio Ravanelli, Gianluca Festa and Brazilians Juninho and Emerson had all been signed to deliver a samba brand of football in the North East, which had managed to claim some big scalps without ever securing long-term success. Middlesbrough had, at the time, never won a professional trophy and this final could have brought to an end twelve decades of hurt. Everyone was aware of Leicester's spirit and fight, but it was widely acknowledged that Boro's star players would thrive on the expansive Wembley turf and rise to the occasion. O'Neill, however, was making a fifth appearance at Wembley in six years as a manager and knew what it took to win a game at the famous old stadium. A goalless 90 minutes sent the game into extra-time and O'Neill's side were left devastated when Italian Ravanelli netted five minutes after the restart. However, Emile Heskey, so often O'Neill's saviour at Leicester, struck less than a quarter-of an-hour later to send the final to a replay at Sheffield Wednesday's Hillsborough stadium.

'We have to consider ourselves lucky to pinch the draw with just seconds to go, but I think we deserved it,' O'Neill said after the game. 'We missed some chances, but I thought we shut Juninho out well and controlled their dangermen skilfully for the most part. Of course, I feel sorry for Bryan and the lads, but my priority is to win this damn thing and today has made us even more determined. We will take some lessons back with us and I hope you will see a better performance from us next time.'

Indeed O'Neill's insistence that his side restrict Middlesbrough's flair players, especially the little Brazilian Juninho, did not sit well with the 'hatchet man' he hired for the job. Pontus Kamaark, a £600,000 signing, did not take to his role with much enthusiasm, commenting in the *Mirror*: 'I apologised to Juninho at the end of the first game. Football is supposed to be entertainment and that means the public are always hoping to see world-class stars like Juninho allowed to express themselves on the field of play. I am good at the man-marking role and if the manager asks me to do it again I will follow his wishes. But it makes me a destroyer of the public's pleasure – and I do not regard that task as a moral act. I cannot really enjoy such a role as the crowd will want to watch Juninho's skills, yet it is necessary for me to prevent him from performing.' Showing his trademark dry wit and lack of tolerance towards disobedient players, O'Neill merely retorted: 'Kamaark can continue any moral debate once he discovers whether he is actually on the team bus travelling to Hillsborough.'

O'Neill kept faith with the same line-up for the

Hillsborough replay on 16 April, and another tight contest again failed to find a winner after 90 minutes. Fortunately for O'Neill, journeyman striker Steve Claridge popped up with a late, late winner to send the travelling Leicester support into raptures. 'I think we deserved a wee break,' he said after the game. 'It could have gone either way, but it was just a matter of keeping going and we got the first break.' It is impossible to tell in football whether you will ever win another trophy, so the first one at a new club is always extra special. 'I cannot put into words this moment,' he told the *Irish Times*. 'It won't take a week to sink in; it won't take a month. If we avoid relegation it will sink in some time during the summer. It is a superb moment for everyone at the football club. The fans have been sensational. It is fantastic, but I feel sorry for Bryan Robson as his side played some great football, but we were great too and deserve this.'

As delighted as he was to have given the Leicester supporters a trophy, O'Neill acknowledged that football supporters can be fickle, and that the sweet taste of success experienced at Wembley would not last forever. He told the *Express*: 'There will be a new generation at Leicester City who wouldn't have a clue and couldn't care what happened when I was there. When Leicester moved to the Walkers Stadium they were getting 30,000 people; that's 10,000 more than were coming to Filbert Street. So I feel there are fans now who wouldn't have any notion of who I was. But I had great times at Leicester. It was a harrowing start when I couldn't win a game, but that stood me in good stead.'

Despite the ecstasy of the cup success, there were still a handful of league fixtures to go, and if they wanted to guarantee their top-flight status Leicester needed to pick up some points. Despite a narrow defeat to Chelsea, the Foxes notched up wins over Sheffield Wednesday, West Ham, Blackburn and drew with Manchester United to finish the season in ninth place – a remarkable achievement for a club newly promoted to the Premier League. By the end of the season, talk of a 'double your money' deal in the press was rife and O'Neill signed a new contract. Chairman Tom Smeaton commented: 'Nobody needs to remind me about the importance of Martin O'Neill to Leicester City's future.'

One of the dangers of negotiating a second season in the Premier League is that you are no longer a surprise package. In the past few seasons, Wigan, Hull and Ipswich have all failed to repeat the same dizzying performances of their debut season. O'Neill was determined Leicester would not follow that trend.

By the start of the 1997/98 season some were still doubting Leicester's ability to remain in the top flight, but O'Neill's ability to get the best out of limited means stood them in good stead for what would be another long, hard slog. After picking up an opening-day win over Aston Villa, O'Neill told the *Independent*: 'Much as I would like us to retain the Coca-Cola Cup and win the UEFA Cup, our first and most important task is to get over the finishing line in the Premiership.'

Leicester's European campaign, a sentence not often uttered in the club's history, began against Atletico Madrid

– a stylish and well-drilled side from the Spanish capital. But Leicester, who under O'Neill had earned a reputation as a team of grafters, and who were good enough to have earned draws against Manchester United and Arsenal in the weeks leading up to the game, feared no one. Ahead of the game, he told *The Times*: 'Before the draw was made, I looked at it two ways. Either get the poorest possible team in the competition, draw them and get through or get one of the really, really major teams and get it over with, although that last bit is a throwaway comment and people should not take it too seriously. I would probably have preferred some minnow and tried to take it all a wee bit further, but now we're there, why not go for it?'

'It's all new for us,' he told the *Independent*. 'It's what you dream about. Previously when we have thought about going into Europe it has been for an end-of-season holiday trip to Majorca, but now we are right up there with the big boys.'

That summer, Atletico had plucked the brilliant Brazilian Juninho from Middlesbrough and he would undoubtedly be looking to get one over Leicester City – the club that had denied him the chance of silverware on Teeside.

Atletico's imposing Vicente Calderon stadium, packed with 60,000 vociferous supporters, can be enough to unnerve many of the world's top footballers. In mid-September though, as the Spanish capital finally began to relinquish its grip on summer, Leicester came and took the game to their opponents; so much so that they took the lead 11 minutes into the match, through Ian Marshall. And so it remained at half-time, with Leicester's defence remaining strong in the face of a red and white battering. Something had to give, however, and, unfortunately, Juninho (unsurprisingly tracked by Pontus Kamaark throughout the course of the match) equalised on 70 minutes. Then, just two minutes later, disaster struck when Italian striker Christian Vieiri netted from the penalty spot to give Atletico the advantage going into the second leg at Filbert Street.

'It has given us a chance to have a go at them with a real atmosphere at Filbert Street,' O'Neill said after the game. 'Some of their players might not be prepared for the rickety old stand and the closeness of our crowd, whatever Juninho may tell them.'

Filbert Street had not seen many European nights in its long history and the visit of Atletico Madrid, boasting a squad worth more than £50million, represented the club's biggest match in recent times. Juninho, Christian Vieir, Kiko and company all made the trip to the East Midlands, with O'Neill hoping the lack of home comforts at Leicester's ground would unsettle them.

'It will be a volatile atmosphere – I would be disappointed if it wasn't – but it is the sort you should want to play in,' he said ahead of the game. 'During my career I have been surprised by the number of people you would expect to come up with the goods who have not produced it on the big occasion. But then there are others who might appear as meek as mice, who make you wonder whether they can take the pressure, but who will pull through and be the strengths on the night. My own experience of Europe will mean I will be able to know how a player is feeling during the course of a game – whether after 25 minutes they have got used to the pace and what is required. But, mentally, especially for players experiencing it for the first time, whatever you tell them will not really count for anything. They have got to go through this experience for themselves and deal with it.'

While many may not have been surprised that Atletico went on to win the tie, the manner of the defeat left a bitter taste in the mouth of Martin O'Neill, who could not believe Leicester were denied credible claims for spot-kicks. He said after the game: 'I am disgusted, absolutely and utterly disgusted. They looked like penalty kicks to me...the referee was desperately poor. You do feel "what's the point?" and that in two days' time people will think it is just sour grapes on your part. But then you think there is a point – to prevent what happened happening again.'

A UEFA investigation followed O'Neill's outburst at French referee Remi Harrel, but it was not about to cool the hotheaded Ulsterman, who would never bite his tongue when facing perceived injustice. Perhaps it was the lawyer in him. In the end, however, UEFA's bosses opted against meting out any punishment.

In October, Leicester began the defence of their Coca-Cola Cup crown and were handed a favourable draw, against Grimsby Town. While some of the Premier League's larger clubs may continue to use the competition as a platform upon which they can blood their younger players, O'Neill insisted he would give the cup his full focus. 'We were very proud to win the trophy,' he told the

Mirror. 'And you can be certain we will be defending it with the utmost vigour. If other clubs like Manchester United and Arsenal want to field weakened teams, for whatever reason, that is their prerogative. I make no comment. What I can state is that no one at Filbert Street will ever undervalue or de-value the Coca-Cola Cup, because we believe it is an important facet in the English football calendar. The Coca-Cola Cup holders have always been guaranteed a place in the UEFA Cup and that is how we want it to stay. How could Leicester City feel otherwise? The Coca-Cola was our springboard into Europe and we have had two exciting games against Atletico Madrid [as a result of it]. Apart from that, the competition has plenty of merit in its own right.'

But any hopes of a repeat performance were soon dashed as Grimsby picked up a convincing 3-1 win on home soil to dump the holders out at the first hurdle.

In late October 1997, following the dismissal of Bryan Hamilton, O'Neill was courted by Northern Ireland to manage the national side. However, Leicester refused the Irish FA permission to talk to their boss, meaning little more came of the speculation. Considering O'Neill had said he would not want to break his Leicester contract, the Irish FA had to move their gaze away from Filbert Street. Although it may have come to nothing, the incident served as another example of the respect O'Neill had built up following a dream year for the Foxes. Leicester chairman Tom Smeaton was publicly forced to warn off the Irish FA, telling the *Mirror*: 'If and when we get a call from Belfast I shall say "thank you, but no thank you!" There is absolutely no chance of Martin going anywhere, whether it is on a part-time or full-time basis. Martin has taken this club a long way in a short time, but there is still some distance to travel. We want Martin to complete the task of building Leicester City into a permanent Premiership force, which is why we negotiated a new three-year contract with him during the summer.'

Leicester endured an indifferent few months in the run-up to Christmas, with disappointing defeats to Southampton and Wimbledon representing a bad few weeks for the Leicester boss. But there was guile in the Foxes side, as shown in the battling 3-3 draw with Newcastle at St James' Park. A 1-0 defeat to Everton on 20 December left O'Neill furious with referee Jeff Winter and he would soon face an FA rap for the confrontation. Hit with a charge of misconduct by the Football Association, O'Neill sought a personal hearing to clear his name. Having escaped punishment from UEFA, O'Neill's boisterous touchline manner had brought him into conflict with English football's upper echelons, and not for the last time.

For Leicester, the year ended with a 1-1 draw at home to Sheffield Wednesday. 'I am heartily sick,' O'Neill remarked after the match. 'A draw is as bad as a defeat. We had loads of chances and could have won 12-2. But you have to remember it has been a fantastic '97 for us and I said to my players: "Let's go out and finish the year in style." There was no problem with their spirit, maybe just their self-confidence.'

The year 1998 began with a rollercoaster ride for

Leicester fans: after picking up four points against Manchester United and Liverpool, including a win at Old Trafford, the Foxes were dumped out of the FA Cup in the fourth round by Crystal Palace. For once, O'Neill's cup magic had failed him. Still Leicester's league form was enough to suggest a European place was not out of the question, meaning there was plenty left to play for at Filbert Street. O'Neill was certainly in no doubt that this was possible, having worked out a points total he believed would see the Foxes competing in Europe again next campaign. Having ended a long winless streak at Old Trafford, O'Neill's Leicester added to their impressive run against the big-guns with a thoroughly professional 2-0 win over Chelsea.

Martin O'Neill was a hugely popular figure not only among the Leicester squad, but also with managers across the Premier League. His animated style of management, with his heart very much on his sleeve, had endeared him to many in English football and, by this stage, few would have called O'Neill's managerial credentials into question, as they had done just months after his appointment. But he also displayed a ruthless streak, as evidenced when Steve Claridge – Leicester's hero when he scored the winning goal in the 1996 play-off final against Crystal Palace to secure the club's return to the Premier League and a hugely popular figure with the club's supporters – was shipped out of Filbert Street in early 1998. O'Neill told the *Leicester Mercury*: 'From the time I put up the team sheet for the opening game of the season against Aston Villa and he was not included, Steve Claridge's heart was not in it. He thought he should have been in the side, but I chose Ian Marshall who, of course, scored a cracking goal to set us off on what was an excellent start to the season. The team as a whole did well, and so did Marshall, so there was no reason to make radical changes to what was a side going very well indeed. I was then very disappointed when Steve virtually downed tools. I like to see players reacting to challenges and fighting their way back into contention. Steve did not appear to me to do that. No one can take away what he had done for this club. Without those very important goals, we would not be where we are today. The fee of £400,000 from Wolves is still great value because we bought him for, eventually, £1.2 million and with us gaining promotion and then winning the Coca-Cola Cup, he has repaid that by a mile.'

O'Neill was no stranger to Claridge's situation, as he had often found himself on the fringes of the Nottingham Forest side when he thought he was worthy of a starting place in the 1970s. However, O'Neill had always been able to force his way back into contention. So while he may have understood Claridge to a point, he could not tolerate a lack of effort on behalf of any player. Claridge joined Portsmouth on loan until the end of the season before moving on to Wolves in the summer.

By April 1998, O'Neill's side had slumped to the bottom half of the league as the dream of European football faded. O'Neill was adamant that the achievement would have made his side the 'Pride of the Midlands' but, unfortunately, Europe proved a step too far, even if only a small one. Leicester came agonisingly close to securing

O'Neill's dream: by the end of the season, a slender six points separated fifth-placed Leeds and O'Neill's Leicester, who finished the season in tenth. Defeat to West Ham on the final day of the season may have left O'Neill to rue missed opportunities, but a solid finish in the Premier League also represented a significant achievement for Leicester, especially given the funds O'Neill had at his disposal. In finishing tenth, they had outperformed clubs (such as Newcastle, Tottenham and Everton) who had both much bigger squads and far more financial clout. In summarising the year, O'Neill told the *Leicester Mercury*: 'There is no doubt we have improved. We have come to terms with the Premiership, anyone who has seen us regularly will tell you that – we have had more possession and have dominated more games this season. I can build on that. I was told there was an amount of money available and, as I have not spent any of the flotation money, there should now be even more. In this division, you have to work hard to stand still, but we want to move on, I hope to help us do that and I am looking forward to spending that money…The lads are done for. They have given everything they had and I am immensely proud of them. Amazingly, we have finished one place lower than last time even though we are six points better off. That just shows you what a tough league the Premiership is. We have had a fine season, our team spirit has been excellent and I hope we can be a better side next time.'

Leicester's strong start to the campaign ended up being crucial to their success and O'Neill confessed that sustaining such form throughout the whole season represented their greatest challenge. 'As far as coming to terms with the Premiership, I am not sure it is something you ever come to terms with,' he told the *Leicester Mercury*. 'The season got off to a really bright start. We had not improved the side by bringing in fifteen or sixteen new players. A couple went out, a couple came in. But we knew it was going to be hard and we dug in very hard from the start. By the time we played Atletico Madrid, we had a decent amount of points on the board. Then we began to struggle around December, but we hung on in there.'

By the end of the campaign, with O'Neill's stock at an all-time high, Scottish giants Celtic began casting envious glances in the direction of Filbert Street. At one stage, O'Neill was even installed as the bookies' favourite to take over at Parkhead, but the project underway at Leicester proved too much of a lure to sway the Ulsterman. It was widely acknowledged that O'Neill was not the type of manager to break a contract when there was unfinished business to be done – Norwich being the notable exception – and any rumours were soon quashed.

There was going to be a change in the boardroom, though. At the end of the year, despite being in the middle of the most successful period in the club's history, chairman Tom Smeaton surprisingly resigned. Smeaton, who came to the club in 1996 and who had been responsible for bringing O'Neill to Filbert Street, had overseen a period of renewed confidence at the club, with plans to move to a new stadium, with the assurance of Premier League football, now a realistic prospect. A stock-market floatation earlier in the year had swelled the

Leicester coffers by around £5 million, but all was not well in the City. Leicester City Football Club PLC shares had lost 50 per cent of their value by the end of the 1998 campaign, Smeaton left and Philip Smith promptly replaced him.

O'Neill's Leicester had endured an indifferent start to the 1998/99 campaign, picking up impressive draws against Manchester United and Arsenal but losing to Middlesbrough and Blackburn. O'Neill had been able to hang on to the majority of his squad and had a settled midfield with Muzzy Izzet, Theo Zagorakis and Neil Lennon. However, much to O'Neill's disappointment, the promised funds to bring in reinforcements had not materialised. There was trouble in the air.

By October, George Graham, the former Arsenal boss, had vacated the Leeds United hot seat and the Elland Road club saw O'Neill as the perfect replacement. An approach was made to bring the Ulsterman to Yorkshire; one that was refused by the Leicester board, who were becoming accustomed to speculation regarding their manager. O'Neill, however, tempted perhaps by the financial muscle of Peter Ridsdale and the Leeds board, thought differently. Although he went out of his way to say he would never break a contract, he did feel as though he had a right to hear the offer on the table. 'I am quite clear in the fact that I am entitled to at least hear what Leeds have to say,' O'Neill told *The Times*. 'I feel I owe it to myself and to my family to do that. Others might have different interpretations on it, but I am perfectly happy in my own mind that I would not be breaking my contract. When I was the manager of Wycombe Wanderers, I had the opportunity to speak to a number of other clubs and when offers were made I turned them down. There is no fait accompli now.'

Leeds were playing hardball and wanted O'Neill installed sooner rather than later. The Elland Road club had finished fifth in the Premier League in 1997/98 and were spending heavily in order to bring success to the club – something that would eventually prove their downfall. The Yorkshire club were also playing in the UEFA Cup and had a mouth-watering tie against AS Roma to look forward to. Ridsdale remained hopeful he could at least have the chance to present his case to O'Neill. 'The rules are that I cannot have a conversation with Martin without approval from Leicester,' he said. 'It is in his and our hands to persuade Leicester that he should be allowed to speak to us. The best thing seems to be for Martin to talk to us and then decide what he wants to do,'

O'Neill was still fighting for what he saw as his right to talk to the Yorkshire club, telling the *Guardian*: 'I had a gentleman's agreement with [board members] Sir Rodney and Mr Elsom that under the circumstances of turning down the vacancy at Everton in the summer I would have the right to talk to other clubs. I have kept quiet long enough. Now is the time for me to come out and say what the situation is. I did not want to make a song and dance about it initially, and at the time of the agreement I did not expect a club of Leeds' stature to come along. I am quite clear that I am entitled, at the very least, to hear what they will have to say. I want permission to talk to Leeds.'

Chairman Elsom promptly denied the existence of any such gentleman's agreement: 'I remember the meeting. It lasted for about an hour and a half, and perhaps 25 seconds was taken up with the matter Martin is referring to. I cannot believe in my wildest imagination that we would change our minds and allow Martin to speak to Leeds. There is a possibility that he could be pushed into walking out of this club, but I feel he and I are close enough to talk it over and reach a satisfactory conclusion.'

It was true that O'Neill had many supporters at Leicester and a good relationship with the board, but the opportunity to manage Leeds, with a clear conscience, was a fantastic opportunity for any manager.

At the time, before financial woes sent the club spiralling down the divisions, the job at Elland Road was one of the most sought after in the Premier League. O'Neill may have insisted that he had no intention of walking out of Leicester, but the principle of the situation clearly irked him. However, when, in a matter of days, Leeds' interest began to wane, O'Neill's open irritation turned to words of calm. He told the *Leicester Mercury*: 'The whole disagreement has been blown up out of all proportion. I don't have rows with John Elsom, just the odd difference of opinion, and I admit I am disappointed at the difference of interpretation on whether I have the right to talk to Leeds. I still believe I have that right and I don't think the fans would begrudge me that right, but right now I have a job to do here in the Premiership. I agreed to stay on in the summer on the condition that certain things would be sorted out politically. This has not happened yet, but I am

not going to walk out, nor is there any intention of me
leaving at the end of the season. Normally I don't say what
happens in our dressing room, but before the season
started we all sat down and I told the players that this was
a hugely important season for the club. We all set out to
give it our best shot and continue the improvement we
have shown over the last two seasons. At that time, we
were also fired by the prospect of playing in a brand new
stadium next season, with facilities equal to other clubs
we have seen building fine grounds. The delay to the plans
has been a big knock-back to us. We also said we would sit
down in the summer to re-evaluate what progress we had
made and if we could take the whole thing further, but at
no stage was that a threat that I might leave.'

However, the process, much to O'Neill's irritation,
continued to drag on. 'It is going on too long, I am
beginning to get fed up with it myself,' he told the
Leicester Mercury. 'It looks as if it is now all down to me
and I have to consider the best decision for all concerned.
So, whatever comes and goes, it is not down to anyone
else, whatever advice they might give me. It is either stay
– or I decide that I go myself to talk with them. So from
that aspect, I just want to give it some thought. The crowd
have been brilliant, a lot more than I could have expected
in many aspects, but I will try to divorce myself from all
that and make a decision one way or the other. Honestly, I
don't want it to carry on any further. I have had a chance
to sleep on it, but I will stick to what I said. By late tonight
the decision will have been made.'

O'Neill's decision to talk freely and openly about the

conflict he was feeling was testament both to his respect for Leicester and a desire to further his career. Had he taken Leicester as far as they could go? Cup success, Premier League survival and a short-lived UEFA Cup run was more than Leicester could have expected two years previously.

A 2-1 win over Tottenham, inspired by midfielder Muzzy Izzet, highlighted the players' determination to keep hold of their inspirational boss and, on 21 October, O'Neill told the *Leicester Mercury*: 'I want to stay at this club. The reaction of the fans on Monday night, plus the hundreds of letters and faxes, has been a big factor in my decision. The determination the players have shown under what were difficult circumstances of uncertainty for them has also played a big part in my choice. The players and I made a pact that we would really give it a crack this season and see how far we can go. Europe was the aim and, after a shaky start, maybe we can still try for it. The chairman Jon Elsom had not given me permission to talk to Leeds and I was disappointed with that on principle, however the option to me was not palatable. It would have meant walking out on my contract even though I would probably have won any legal argument on it. That was not a choice I would have wanted to pursue. Who knows if any opportunity like the Leeds job will come round again? My disappointment was only that I was not allowed to speak to them, but it is now all over and you won't hear a murmur from me about any other club from now on.

'The situation was not of my making,' he continued. 'I didn't want it to drag on so long. I never intended for it to

76

go all the way down to me having the choice of staying or having to walk out and I was not going to leave the club under those circumstances. On the other aspect of interference from the commercial side, this was not an unfounded argument and, on that matter, I will be expecting Mr Elsom and Sir Rodney Walker to keep their part of the bargain very strictly this time. Mr Elsom has put a very substantive contract in front of me, but I will not be signing it until I can see that certain things have been sorted out. I do not want any more interference in football matters at all.'

Elsom, for his part, was happy to take some responsibility in the very public washing of dirty laundry at Filbert Street. He told the *Leicester Mercury*: 'As for the demarcation disputes between the commercial and playing sides, I would take responsibility for eradicating that. Obviously I did not do my job well enough in the summer and it is fair to say I had misunderstood the depth of Martin's feeling on the matter. It is for me to ensure that relationships will be sorted out, but that does not mean it will necessarily be changed in terms of personnel. My fear was that they would roll out the red carpet and we might lose him. I don't think he has been betrayed in terms of the gentleman's agreement. We disagree on the interpretation of what was said in the summer and I stuck to the stance I had taken.'

O'Neill admitted that he had not forgotten the support Elsom had given him in the early stages of his Leicester career. 'Three years ago, when there was not a lot of support for me at boardroom level, Mr Elsom chose to vouch for the fact that I would get it right in time. I have a great respect for the blind allegiance he showed at that time and my relationship with him will not change. This should finally end the whole matter. I now want to get on with the job I have here, which is to continue winning as many matches as possible.' His words did little to dampen the speculation regarding his future when the hot seat at the City Ground, 30 miles up the road from Leicester, became available.

With his future now secure O'Neill could begin to focus on bringing both league and cup success to the club. Gone were the days when Premier League survival was enough for the Foxes faithful. The standards had been set and constant improvements would be needed.

The media speculated that O'Neill was not entirely comfortable in his decision to stay at Filbert Street. In his column in the *Belfast Newsletter*, Alan Green commented: 'To me, there was nothing in what Martin O'Neill said, or in his body language, to suggest that he was particularly happy with his decision to stay at Filbert Street. Simply, this was a case of an honourable man agreeing to abide by his contract, but do not be fooled into believing all is now well. He admits being naïve thinking Leicester City would themselves abide by an unwritten agreement forged during the summer when the manager was considering the then vacancy at Everton. Namely that the club would allow him to talk to any "bigger" clubs that were interested in his services. As Martin says, having studied law at Queen's University, he should have known better.'

Few stories better encapsulate the love Foxes fans had

for Martin O'Neill than the appreciation showed by one Leicester school once he decided to stay. A huge banner with the words 'Thanks Martin for Staying' was hung outside Sacred Heart Primary School, in Spinney Hills. Headteacher Pat Mendes told the *Leicester Mercury*: 'I am a lifelong Leicester City fan and I had the most miserable couple of weeks of my life when I thought he was going to go to Leeds. Whenever I led the prayers in assembly I made them pray for Leicester City. Martin O'Neill has got to do so much out of nothing. We added up the value of his squad and it is less than one Manchester United player.'

O'Neill would reward the Leicester fans with another campaign ending at Wembley in the New Year, but, by the end of October 1998, as the Fox's impressive form continued, the immediate reward was a 1-0 home win over Roy Evans' Liverpool. O'Neill feared his squad would tail off like the year before and issued a rallying call to his players as the season moved into November. He told the *Leicester Mercury*: 'We actually have less points than we had last time. After nine games, we had eighteen points and now we have sixteen from eleven, but we got stuck in the twenties for a long time [last season]. The next ten games will be crucial for us. By the twentieth, which is Blackburn at home, we would like to be around the thirty mark. That means fourteen points out of the next nine games, which I would say is title-challenging form. Last season, at this stage, we didn't do so well. Perhaps it was the aftermath to going out of Europe against Atletico Madrid and also falling at the first hurdle in our defence of the Coca-Cola Cup. Having tasted Europe not so long ago, the target is very much in our thoughts. I have set a points target for the next group of games and it will determine whether Europe will still be a target or if we need to look over our shoulder.'

O'Neill was rewarded for his efforts with the Premier League Manager of the Month award for October, an accolade known to be something of a poisoned chalice, as it has often heralded a considerable downturn in form for a recipient's team. 'All I know is that I am delighted to receive the prize on behalf of the players whose efforts have been the cause of it all,' said the Leicester manager. He was also buoyed by key players pledging their future to the club as the prospect of Leicester becoming a permanent top-half proposition looked ever more likely.

By November Peter Ridsdale had become the victim of a hate mob campaign on the Elland Road terraces and the chairman was given a taste of what he could have had as Leeds travelled to Filbert Street for an emotionally charged match, which the Foxes eventually won by two goals to one. A first defeat in ten games did come at the hands of West Ham, but overall Leicester had performed admirably during a spell in which they had struggled the year before. Rather than be a hindrance, questions over O'Neill's future had in fact galvanised the squad and brought about some excellent results.

Behind the scenes there was also cause for optimism, at least on the part of Leicester City plc chairman Sir Rodney Walker. 'Since I came here a year ago there have been stresses and strains and I have worked hard to reduce them and remove them,' he told the *Leicester Mercury*. 'Relationships are improving – this week Barrie Pierpoint has accepted a new contract and he will oversee the development of the new stadium and Martin O'Neill was given a copy of a new contract on Wednesday.'

When asked about the uneasy truce, O'Neill refused to offer the easy answer: 'I want to run the football club the way I see fit,' he said. 'I think I know more about football than these people, so I will live and die by my results. You ask me will the problems ever be overcome – I think you must ask other people. But I believe, if I am left alone, then I will do a good job for this club. I think the board just about tolerate me – but once the results start to go against me I am done here. To walk away after blackmailing some players to stay would have been too difficult to stomach.' Plans for Leicester's new stadium were pushing ahead but, as he had stated before, O'Neill's preference would have been to extend Filbert Street, a tough, uncompromising stadium that got the best out of his players.

By Christmas, Leicester were in the final four of the Worthington Cup (the re-branded League Cup), with a tie against First Division leaders Sunderland in the offing. Leicester City were reaping the rewards of getting O'Neill to stay at Filbert Street, but the manager remained convinced that more off-the-field support was needed to propel the club to further glories. 'The hard core of our side is very strong, but the only way for us to bridge the gap with the top clubs is to go on and win some more trophies,' he told the *Daily Mail*. 'A new stadium and the extra revenue it can bring would go towards helping us keep our best players. We have got players who would grace bigger clubs and our problem is trying to keep them. Heskey has a big future and I would like it to be at Leicester for as long as possible, but we need to be successful.'

The double-headed semi-final against Sunderland began at the Stadium of Light; O'Neill was sure of what he wanted going into the game. 'It is easy to talk about the usual things,' he told the *Leicester Mercury*, 'like the importance of grabbing an away goal or showing there is a gap between the First Division and the Premiership. But I can tell you this: I am only looking for us still being in with a chance to take into the next game. The last thing I want is for us to be coming back down the motorway virtually out of the competition and with little hope of turning things round at Filbert Street. That, for me, would be the worse scenario. The so-called gap in status, for me, does not exist. We had people watching Sunderland at Blackburn last Saturday and our reports suggest they were unlucky not to win. They have hardly lost any games in a long run and they will be backed by tremendous support in a great stadium. They are Premiership in all but name and look as if they will be joining the top flight in the summer anyway.'

A 2-1 win at the Stadium of Light was certainly more than O'Neill had hoped for, at least in public, as Leicester once again proved their cup credentials. 'It was very quiet in the dressing room; no shouting, no congratulations, no sense of elation,' he told *The Times*. 'Perhaps I wish that the game had been decided tonight.'

In between the two legs, O'Neill swooped to secure the signing of forward Arnar Gunnlaugsson for £2 milion, while at the same time casting a jealous eye over similar clubs splashing out upwards of £7 million. John Hartson, who would later join O'Neill at Celtic, made a big-money move to Wimbledon, much to the Ulsterman's chagrin. 'I would have liked to have been in a position of affording everything to do with the John Hartson transfer, both the fee and his wages,' he told the *Leicester Mercury*. 'I think he is a great player, but we simply could not afford him and that is something that I have a big concern about. If it had been up to me, I would have tried to scrape up all the money to sign Hartson because I think it would have helped this club. To put it plain and simply, if Wimbledon can afford to sign him and pay his wages, then we should most certainly be able to. It does not mean I would spend £7.5 million just to prove a point. It is the ability to do so.'

A 1-1 draw at Filbert Street against Sunderland in the second leg of the Worthington Cup semi-final, while not a roaring statement of intent, proved enough to give Leicester a Wembley appearance. 'It feels every bit as good as last time,' O'Neill beamed. Leicester's on-the-field success had delayed O'Neill in signing a new contract, which he insisted would happen soon. He told the *Leicester Mercury*: 'I have already said I will sign and that is true, I would be foolish not to. But in my view there have been far more important issues going on. For instance, we had to fix up Robbie Savage on a new contract and we are negotiating for Pontus Kaamark and Rob Ullathorne to follow. We had to sign Arnar

Gunnlaugsson, and, of course, there was the little matter of a Worthington Cup semi-final to deal with. I understand it is not yet a fait accompli and there are a few things still to be sorted out before it can be definite. But what is definite is that we do need a new stadium somewhere if we are to take this whole thing forward.'

Tottenham Hostpur waited in the Worthington Cup final in what would be a tough game for the Foxes. Spurs' insatiable supporters had been starved of glory for almost a decade and the League Cup represented their first taste of success since winning the FA Cup in 1991. For O'Neill it was a massive game. 'It would be fantastic to repeat what we did two years ago – winning at Wembley will mean everything to me. We have got 32,000 people following us to Wembley in the hope of us winning the game and I will do the best I can to win the cup.'

The Leicester manager's preparations for the crunch showpiece were dealt a blow when defender Frank Sinclair failed to show for a team meeting and was quickly ejected from the squad. O'Neill told the *Daily Mail*: 'Frank was unable to provide me with a satisfactory explanation. Like several other players he was given permission to leave our hotel and go to the cinema. The rest of the players arrived back on time, but he did not. I assume he did not suffer a heart attack at the cinema, so there was no good reason for him to have been late. It was very disappointing and cost the club dearly in terms of attitude.'

He continued in the *Leicester Mercury*: 'Frank was very contrite and accepted he was in the wrong, but he could hardly complain because there was absolutely no excuse. We had a team meeting arranged for a certain time and twenty-three out of our twenty-four-man squad were all there, including players who, because they were ineligible or injured, knew they were not going to be playing. And I have to say Frank had, at that stage, as good a chance as anyone of being picked in the side because, apart from Rob Ullathorne being told he would be on [facing] David Ginola, the team had not been picked. I think Frank learned his lesson. He has accepted he was in the wrong, accepted his punishment and seems genuinely sorry for what he did. That's good enough for me.'

With Sinclair sent packing, the final, at a rain-soaked Wembley in February, was far from a classic – cup finals seldom are. But with minutes left on the clock, and Leicester holding a man advantage following Justin Edinburgh's red card, O'Neill told his troops to hold out until extra-time. Unfortunately, they were unable to keep the ball for the dying minutes and an Allan Neilson strike broke Leicester hearts. Rather than help his team, O'Neill felt the sending-off had heralded a turn for the worse. Leicester had been dominant at the time of Edinburgh's red card, but had failed to make their man advantage count as Spurs closed up and hoped to hit them on the break. A disappointed O'Neill told the *Independent*: 'In the first half one side negated the other, but from a tactical viewpoint I was happy with it. But it is all about winning.'

Within a matter of weeks Leicester had avenged their Worthington Cup final pain with a 2-0 win over Spurs at White Hart Lane and, although there had been no silverware on the line on this occasion, O'Neill knew the importance of maintaining momentum in the league if Leicester stood a chance of mounting a challenge for a European spot. Three consecutive score draws followed (against Aston Villa, West Ham and Chelsea) before, in late April, a trip to Anfield gave the injury-hit Foxes a true test of their European credentials. They were not found wanting, picking up a 1-0 victory courtesy of Ian Marshall's last-gasp effort.

'It was terrific to take all three points and no doubt we will have loftier targets ahead,' O'Neill told the *Leicester Mercury*. 'That is just me getting carried away as usual, but I have to say some of our football was brilliant. If you had said that, without the likes of Muzzy Izzet, Steve Walsh, Gerry Taggart, we would have managed a draw and a victory in the two big games against top-class opponents in Chelsea and Liverpool I would not have believed it. Confidence is sweeping through the squad at the moment and rightly so. Our safety is not an iron-cast certainty. Sometimes that backfires on you, but I had had confidence in the team.'

However, after that victory at Liverpool O'Neill's team could only muster another six points in their last five games of the season, picking up wins against Coventry and Newcastle, while Southampton and Nottingham Forest both left Filbert Street with three points and the Foxes lost 2-1 to East Midland rivals Derby. As a result Leicester finished the season in tenth place, not enough to see them qualify for Europe and a disappointing end to a season in which they had showed enough quality to compete with the Premier League's established order.

O'Neill told the *Leicester Mercury*: 'The one thing you can always be sure about the Premiership is that it gets more difficult every year. The aims stay the same. Our first target is always to ensure we will be playing at the same level the following season. And for clubs like us, that will always be the main thing. Next, there are the cups and places in Europe to go for. We nearly made it at Wembley this time and, looking at the table now and remembering our bad spell in mid-season, we can see how close we might have come to Europe with a bit more consistency.'

A massive coup for O'Neill in the summer of 1999 was convincing highly rated striker Emile Heskey to sign improved terms at Filbert Street. Heskey had been courted by many of the Premier League's top clubs, but, at least for the meantime, the forward saw his future in the Midlands.

After the Worthington Cup final in the spring the Football Association announced plans to investigate some Leicester players after it was alleged allocated tickets found their way onto the black market. Striker Tony Cottee was named as part of the investigations. 'This business has hurt me so badly,' the veteran striker told the *Mirror*. 'My name has been smeared for no good reason. There was absolutely no trouble in the section of the stadium for which I received tickets, so I don't understand what it is that is supposed to make me guilty of any offence. I provided tickets for my best friend, who supports Tottenham, plus my accountant and his two young boys. That is all. The publicity surrounding this unfortunate matter has had a terrible effect.'

O'Neill himself added: 'There is absolutely no

suggestion of any tickets being sold over the odds. The FA maintain that the individuals concerned failed to fill in forms detailing where their tickets went before a stated deadline. I can say categorically, and I have the evidence, there was no such deadline. We are all tarnished by this. All of this hassle could have been avoided if there had been some sort of dialogue. But the players and staff at this training ground knew nothing of any deadline. They were told by the FA's compliance officer, Graham Bean, when he came down on 3 August with the forms to fill them in "at your convenience". The next thing they know, a deadline has been and gone and their names are all over the papers with headlines such as "Club of Shame". We have now got to live with it. The FA are trying to make an example of Leicester City and I don't like it. They have got things wrong, and so have one or two people at our end in terms of administration. I should have headed up this enquiry at the Filbert Street end from the very start, then perhaps none of this would ever have happened. Personally, although I am not directly involved, I feel upset and angry. If anyone can prove any ticket-touting stemming from Leicester, I will impose severe penalties.'

Leicester's inability to get plans for their new stadium finalised, even though the start of the 2000/01 season was less was than twelve months away, left the club's board in turmoil. Bitter infighting threatened to tear the club apart and the trench warfare behind the scenes certainly rankled with the club's boss. Sir Rodney Walker and John Elsom were involved in bitter struggle with chief executive Barrie Pierpoint. Three of the club's commercial staff were suspended. After a meeting less than twenty-four hours before a match against Sunderland, O'Neill spoke out, telling the *Mirror*: 'It was a totally inappropriate time for this meeting in the first place. I had to attend at 6pm when I should have been preparing my players for a game at Sunderland. I regard this whole business as a really serious matter. It is something of a very grave nature to myself and the club.'

PLC chairman Sir Rodney added: 'There are divisions within this club which are long standing and deep rooted. In the past two years, I have tried without success to persuade people to work together in the best interests of Leicester City.' Sir Rodney had stormed out of the summit meeting after a statement he found 'totally unacceptable'.

O'Neill had already admitted Leicester's reputation lay in tatters after being dragged through the mud following the Worthington Cup final affair, but at least on the pitch everything was going okay for the Foxes. 'I have worked hard at the club for four years and I am not going to give that up,' the Leicester manager continued. 'But the political matter has not been resolved. It is not tolerable and cannot continue. While this situation exists the club cannot go forward, it is farcical, maybe even worse than that.'

On the pitch, Leicester had started the 1999/2000 season strongly, picking up impressive draws against Liverpool and Chelsea and winning four of their opening nine fixtures, including an emphatic 3-0 victory away at Middlesbrough. Following a convincing 3-1 win over Aston Villa, O'Neill admitted the club's squabbling board could learn from the players. He told the *Independent*: 'These boys come here amid all the boardroom wrangling and produce a performance like that and sometimes I think the directors should have a wee look at it. This game is about the supporters and the players.'

Claims and counter claims regarding the future of Leicester City plc chairman Sir Rodney Walker caused a massive power struggle in the club, with Sir Rodney maintaining he still held his post at the club and rival directors claiming he had resigned a month previously. O'Neill who, by mid-October, had taken Leicester to fifth in the table, had made it abundantly clear his allegiance lay with Walker and Elsom. The boardroom wrangling also delayed the arrival of the financial backing that had been earmarked for investment in the squad. O'Neill told the *Leicester Mercury*: 'I understand that our lenders are reluctant to commit themselves while all this trouble is going on. This inevitably has an effect on any plans I might have and I do have a target or two in my mind that I would like to try to bring to this club. I am not saying that players I might have wanted have gone elsewhere because of the internal wrangling. The targets would not know they were targets for a start. But what does concern me is that a deal that suits us and that could be done might not happen until the boardroom issue is sorted out. No one will lend us the money for new players, something I still maintain we need.'

O'Neill was honoured for his efforts with the Manager of the Month award for November after suffering only one loss – against Manchester United. In the boardroom, Gary

Martin O'Neill signed for Nottingham Forest in 1971. Here he is at a photocall for their successful 1978/79 season.

Above: Nottingham Forest's Martin O'Neill runs at Ipswich Town's Paul Mariner at Portman Road on 3 March, 1979.

Right: Martin played an integral role in Nottingham Forest's promotion to the top flight league.

Above: Brian Clough, Nottingham Forest manager (*centre*) leads his team in singing on the coach to Birmingham. Martin O'Neill is in the third row, second from right.

Below: The Forest team in 1979. Martin is in the front row, second from right.

Above: Martin in action for Norwich City in 1982.

Below: He also had a brief stint playing for Manchester City.

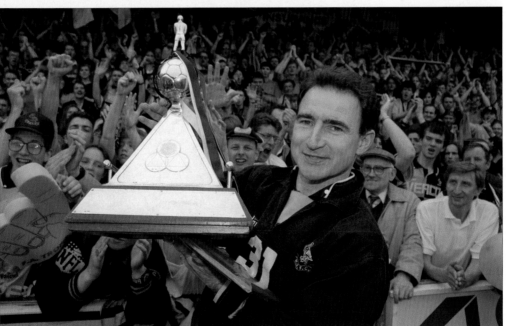

Above: After beginning his managerial career at Grantham Town and Shepshed Dynamo, Martin became the manager of Wycombe Wanderers FC in 1990.

Below: Martin celebrates winning promotion into the Football League with the Wanderers in 1993.

Martin shouts instructions to his Leicester City team at Wembley.

Lifting the trophy with Leicester City at the Worthington Cup Final in February 2000.

Above: Martin raises a green-and-white Celtic scarf high in the air after he is named their new manager in June 2000.

Below: Overseeing a Celtic training session.

Lineker, a major shareholder at Leicester, and one of the club's most revered figures, showed his support for the Elsom/Walker pairing. O'Neill, meanwhile, went as far as to say that he could quit the club if the 'gang of four' headed by Barrie Pierpoint, won control at Filbert Street. He told the *Daily Record*: 'There has been a suggestion that I would be offered the role of Director of Football if the gang of four win. I am not interested in that idea – my only interest at the moment is in sending out a side that continues to do well for Leicester City. Since our opening-day defeat at Highbury, we have taken twenty-nine points from fifteen league matches – that is the sort of average that can win a title. Perhaps people should realise what we have achieved against the odds.'

O'Neill's concerns about friction in the boardroom were matched by the lack of progress on the new stadium, which looked unlikely to be ready before 2002 when initial projections had been aiming for 2000. The club was being hampered by the capacity of Filbert Road. Leicester were one of only two clubs with average gates of less than 30,000 (the other being West Ham) to finish in the top half of the table for three years. Comparing the Foxes with Derby, a club of similar size, O'Neill noted that their attendances had risen from 18,000 to 29,000 with the move to Pride Park. A decent stadium and large crowds attracted new players as well as increased gate receipts. 'The new stadium is being delayed and there is a lack of stability,' he told the *Independent*. 'That is why I have been so pleased with the effort of the players on the pitch – that is where a football club does its talking.'

It was widely regarded that the Leicester board's very public airing of their dirty laundry had detracted from the players' – and manager's – achievements in the first half of the season. However, by the end of 1999, a new board looked to be put in place. Certainly O'Neill hoped the bitter feud would now be at an end and that he would be backed by a team of united directors willing to agree and invest in the squad – which was already punching well above its weight thanks to an inspirational boss. By late December three of the so-called 'gang of four', Gilbert Kinch, Phil Smith and Roy Parker resigned days before Christmas. The situation O'Neill described as 'something he would rather not contemplate' had passed and the partnership of John Elsom and Sir Rodney Walker had won the battle for control of Leicester.

Director Phil Smith made his feelings about O'Neill's allegiance clear. He felt the manager's decision to pick sides during the squabble, and to stick very firmly to the side he had chosen, had undermined the gang of four's challenge for control. In a statement, Smith said:

> The shareholders of Leicester City plc have been asked who they want to govern their company at an EGM – and from the proxy of votes cast it is clear that the vote is likely to go against us. It is with the best interest of Leicester City FC in mind that three of us, Mr Parker, Mr Kinch and myself, have chosen not to contest the resolutions which call for our removal from the board at the EGM. With immediate effect, we three resign from the board of Leicester City plc.

However, our resignations should not be misconstrued as an admission that we have done anything wrong. On the contrary, we believe we have worked in the best long-term interests of the club. We accept that our shareholders are our jury, but on this occasion we firmly believe the jury is wrong. We are acutely aware that the public opinion has been directed against us because the real issues have been presented by the media as a straightforward choice between Martin O'Neill and ourselves. It does not appear to matter that Sir Rodney Walker and John Elsom have offered no reasonable explanation, either, for the Worthington Cup tickets fiasco. They have also sought to confuse the position regarding their resignations by emphasising that they did not put anything in writing. They have instead chosen to hide behind the support of Martin O'Neill who has left no one in doubt as to his position and the possible consequences if we had won the vote. At no time has Martin O'Neill told us any concrete reasons as to why he is not able to work with us. On the other hand, we have continually demonstrated our willingness to work with Martin O'Neill and have provided him with every reasonable financial and organisational comfort that his future lies with Leicester City FC.

Our board has made Martin O'Neill one of the highest paid managers in British football. We have on several occasions provided funds to break the club's record transfer fee. The latest of these was only last week when we provided £3 million for the purchase of Darren Eadie. We are totally committed to relocating the club to a new state-of-the-art stadium, gaining the full support of our city council, club sponsors and ensuring a facility to match Martin O'Neill's stated ambitions. I put it to you: does this demonstrate any lack of support for our manager? Throughout we have given our full support to Leicester City's chief executive Barrie Pierpoint and our support for him remains. Unlike ourselves, Barrie Pierpoint is under contract as an employee of Leicester City and he will not be resigning because this would be a breach of his new contract. However, it is clear from the proxy votes cast that his removal from the board is likely. We hope he will be treated fairly by the new board and the shareholders and the fans. Our departure from the board should offer comfort to the fans and shareholders, and ensure that, after his strong support for Sir Rodney Walker and John Elsom, Martin O'Neill will not leave Leicester City FC until at least the end of his contract in 2002 irrespective of the clauses he has insisted were in it. We would now expect at least that of him.

We are leaving Leicester City in the knowledge that we have done our best for the club – and with the club in good shape. We are currently in sixth place in the Premiership and within sight of a third major Wembley final in four years.

So a very public swipe at Martin O'Neill had landed, but

the Ulsterman, of course, side-stepped the blow. He told the *Leicester Mercury*: 'They brought it on themselves. I am only the football manager, only an employee and I did not start proceedings. My support for John Elsom stems from the fact that, in my opinion, he genuinely has the good of the football club at heart. I also now feel the football side of matters will be the priority.'

So, as one national newspaper put it, football had won at Filbert Street, but the players were unable to show any of their newfound relief with success on the pitch. Consecutive defeats to Derby, Newcastle and Leeds saw Leicester go into the new millennium in a bad run of form and they would have to wait until February for their first league win of the New Year. The spell ranked as O'Neill's worst run of results at the club and saw the club's European ambitions take a real hit. Success in cup competition, however, was still forthcoming. After a goalless first match against Arsenal in the fourth round of the FA Cup, another stalemate heralded the dreaded penalty shootout, which O'Neill's men won 6-5 to claim a mighty scalp in the competition. Buoyed by this, the Foxes secured a return to Wembley by hitting the only goal in a tense two-legged Worthington Cup semi-final with Aston Villa and as a result would face unfancied Tranmere Rovers in the final.

As part of the team's final preparations they were flown out to a specialist training centre in La Manga, Spain. O'Neill had stayed behind in England but, on the very first night, the behaviour of the squad hit the headlines. In particular Stan Collymore, the brilliant former

Liverpool striker O'Neill had signed in the hope of recapturing former glories. Managing director of La Manga, Tony Coles, told the *Leicester Mercury*: 'We have had over 250 teams visit our soccer centre since it was opened in 1998 and we have never had any problems whatsoever. We were looking forward to the arrival of Leicester City, an exciting team who are doing great things in the Premier League. It is extremely regrettable that through the first evening the team were here, when they were clearly enjoying themselves, one of the players, Stan Collymore, let off a fire extinguisher in a public bar, which is unacceptable behaviour. As a consequence, after discussions with the coaches and with Martin O'Neill, we demanded the team leave.'

O'Neill's response to the news was stern: 'They will have to incur my wrath. Reports coming back from Spain are a bit sketchy, but I will find out what has happened and speak to the people involved.'

As a result of his actions, Collymore was hit with a fine of two weeks' wages and a warning over his future conduct. 'In footballing parlance, I would say it's a yellow card,' the Leicester manager told the *Daily Record*. 'If he is on a yellow card, I would say he is in severe danger of losing his job. Did I consider sacking Stan? I have got to say that when he came here I thought he would perhaps be involved in an incident in some way in his first six or seven weeks here that would make me start to think, "Is this a sacking offence?" I didn't expect it to happen so quickly, but I personally believe that this was not a sacking offence. Unless it was incredibly serious, in other words where some other person might have been hurt, then I didn't think it was a sackable offence. I believe that setting off a fire extinguisher and causing £700 worth of damage to carpets, settees, people's suits and so on, is not a sacking offence. But it is a warning. Those people who voiced concerns about the wisdom of taking him on will probably say, "I told you so" – and at the moment I could not argue with them. I still believe it is a risk worth taking, but I would have to say the events will perhaps suggest to me that I need my head examining!'

So Leicester City again found themselves in the spotlight for matters unrelated to football. Stan Collymore, though, could not see what all the fuss was about. In an interview with the *Leicester Mercury* in 2009, he said: 'Signing for Martin O'Neill at Leicester was great because he was the best manager I played under. Martin had stressed to me, though, when I arrived that I needed to keep my nose clean. I could not quite believe that within a week or two I found myself in the middle of one of the biggest footballing news stories and we were even the first item on *News at Ten*. The events have been written into folklore but, at the time, it seemed like nothing more than a light-hearted joke to let off the extinguisher.'

Leicester's achievements, with an injury-ravaged squad, may have been remarkable, but their ability to grind out results had left some accusing them of anti-football – with then Chelsea chairman Ken Bates a leading and vocal critic of Leicester's solid approach to the game. O'Neill, predictably, launched a firm defence of his players. After a narrow defeat to Chelsea in the FA Cup, O'Neill fumed in the *Belfast Newsletter*: 'On top of everything you get footballing cretins like Ken Bates writing in his programme notes that we have come along and played for penalties. If that's the case he doesn't know his facts. In the two times we have been to Wembley we have never actually had penalties or extra-time or replays. So he has got that wrong. We played Chelsea here two weeks ago and played them off the pitch. We should have scored five or six. He must not have been at that game. He must have been inside a Chinese restaurant or something.'

A 2-1 win over Middlesbrough at Filbert Street brought three welcome points but could not kickstart a run of results, and a 1-1 draw at Watford was the best the Foxes could muster before going into the Worthington Cup final. O'Neill admitted his squad had been 'performing miracles' to get to where they were, but that one last push was needed to secure more silverware. Ahead of the game, he gave an interview with the *Irish Times*, revealing a little more of his character. 'There is a paradox between the two sides of my nature. Sometimes the emotional moment is more decisive than the analytical moment. I think I have got a decent, logical brain. It does not ever go to plan. Sometimes you can have two plans for a match and the game follows a third plan. Sometimes I actually have a sore head at the end of a match thinking about all the things which might have materialised.'

Speaking of his where he saw his career going after an inauspicious start to life at Filbert Street, he added: 'I was getting letters saying: "What is happening to our Leicester City?" and I was thinking: "The same as usual, it is steeped in mediocrity." At the end of the season when we got promoted it was delightful for me to call them and get my own back. That is something only a man who had lost his senses would do, but I had lost mine. It was not really normal behaviour. But after a dodgy beginning I have loved it here.'

Skipper Matt Elliot was the unlikely hero at Wembley, netting twice either side of a David Kelly goal to bring the League Cup back to Filbert Street. On his way up to collect the trophy, O'Neill stopped to share a few words with his former boss, Brian Clough – 'I was surprised when I saw him [Clough],' O'Neill told *The Times*. 'But I was delighted'.

He continued in the *Belfast Times*: 'I am thrilled to bits for the players and the club – and I am reasonably pleased for myself! This means a great deal. In the past couple of seasons we have reached three finals and won two of them and in terms of the size of the club we have done splendidly. Winning this competition at Wembley is just about as good a feeling as you are likely to get. But it is also fantastic that we are in Europe now and that part will probably sink in after a few days.'

But while the main aim of league success had already been achieved, O'Neill was not about to let his side get complacent. 'We still have a lot to play for and a place in the top six is certainly within our reach with thirteen games left,' he told the *Leicester Mercury*. 'The top five have opened up a gap, but only six points separate sixth place and twelfth. A couple of good results and you can go up several places; a few defeats and you can drop into the bottom half. We have celebrated winning at Wembley, but now we return to the main competition of the Premiership. It is nice to have won something and to be in Europe already, but there is still work to do. I know this is me being my usual pessimistic self when I say that, for a start, we need a few more points to be mathematically sure of Premiership survival. Yes, I want that forty-two-point tally which should mean safety as quickly as possible, but, of course, I want us to do a lot better than that, and I am sure we can. The top five have risen above the pack, but as for the rest of the teams just below that mark, I believe we are every bit as good as them when we have everyone fit and I see no reason why, in the thirteen games left, we cannot finish at the top of that little group.'

Despite defeats against Manchester United, Derby and Spurs, Leicester ended the season on a high with three wins in their last four games, including a 2-0 win at Anfield. However, the final day of the season, in what would turn out to be O'Neill's last game at the club, saw a 4-0 defeat to already-relegated Sheffield Wednesday on. 'We just had no energy out there,' he told the *Leicester Mercury*, 'which is not like us at all. We played poorly and deserved exactly what we got, which was nothing. I felt sorry for our fans who had travelled up to support us in such great numbers, but to get it all in perspective this was a one-off and we have still had a fabulous season. It is such a pity it should end on this note, but it should not detract from what we have done over the whole season.'

So with eighth place secure, and the call from north of

the border too strong to resist, O'Neill and Leicester City would soon part company. The fans, who had supported and loved him over the past five years, would soon lose the most successful manager in the club's history. O'Neill later reflected on the night the Leicester fans convinced him to stay following the Leeds affair. He told the *Leicester Mercury*: 'It was a really poignant night. I don't want to make too big a deal out of it but yes, that night, the crowd made my mind up for me. We'd had our early skirmishes, but then they grew to like me. The feeling was mutual and I felt we were level again.'

He concluded in the *Irish Times*: 'I would not want to leave the profession without having won a championship. It is really nice and pleasing when people say it is a big achievement to have done what I have at Leicester, but I don't believe a word of it. Every manager in the country will eventually be judged by what they win. I will not be considered top of the tree unless I win a championship.' It appeared he was increasingly unsure that this sort of success could be achieved at Leicester City.

After five hugely successful years, O'Neill and Leicester parted ways having seen their stocks rise respectively. He told the *Leicester Mercury*: 'My two girls had a phenomenal time during our five years in Leicester. I am still good friends with many people there. I didn't fall out with everyone there; it just sometimes felt [as though] I did. But as JF Kennedy once said, the torch passes on. It is up to someone else. But I loved it there. I had five of the best years of my life there.'

At Leicester, O'Neill admitted he had struggled to get

football out of his head, often at the cost of his family. He told *The Times*: 'I don't find it easy to relax away from the game. Most boys pick up golf and things like this here and that type of stuff, but I don't. I can't. I haven't got an ability to be able to relax at the end of it all. I would love to be able to do it and I do envy managers who, once they step into their car to go home, the game no longer counts for them. Well, I am not one of those, unfortunately. My two daughters and my wife have to listen to me persistently about this and about that, about the game. And when they come in and put a point of view and I don't agree with that point of view, then it's bedlam and it goes on forever. I can't do it. I can't let it go. That has been the story in our household for a number of years. I have got plenty of other interests, don't worry about that, but football is never that far away. Even as a player, funnily enough, I was always last out of the dressing room, still contemplating the game. That is just the way I am, unfortunately, and at some stage I really should wise up. If somebody could tell me how to do it, I would. People turn around and say to me: "Have you mapped your career out?" I have got to say to you, as a typical Irishman, that I have never mapped a day out, never mind anything else. If you are trying to plan a career, good luck to you, but if you are trying to plan a career in football management, forget about it, it is an impossibility. When I first came to Leicester, I copped a load of hassle and if you had seen the situation in January '97 when I had not won any of my first ten games in charge and there was hell to pay, you would be surprised. But I wanted to see the job through. I don't like to leave and think I have only done half a job. It has gone well since, but it was precarious. I don't fashion out a career. I just do everything I possibly can where I am so that at least I can turn around and say: "I worked my guts out to do this and I was worth every penny someone paid me."'

CHAPTER 6

FROM MEN
TO BHOYS

'I know one day the 60,000 will be baying for my blood –
I am sure in the course of time that will happen. Managers will
come and go, so will the players, but the fans won't.'

To understand just how monumental Celtic's treble-winning 2000/01 season was for both the club and for Martin O'Neill, it is important to understand the factors leading up to the campaign. Celtic had endured a manager merry-go-round in recent years, made all the worse by in-form Rangers scooping top honours in the SPL. Liverpool and England favourite John Barnes was the latest to try his hand at Parkhead, but the club still finished a massive twenty-one points behind Rangers. The board and fans alike were in need of some stability not only to stop the rot, but to form, once again, a side that could wrestle the title from their near neighbours across the River Clyde. At Leicester, O'Neill had enjoyed a fantastic 1999/2000 season, finishing the season in eighth place above established big clubs such as West Ham, Tottenham and

Newcastle. O'Neill's charisma, energy and results had made him hot property in Britain and few doubted whether he would make a move away from Filbert Street; the only questions being when and where.

O'Neill's name was touted for the Old Firm role but, if the tabloids are to be believed, he was not first choice for the job. According to the *Mirror*, former Real Madrid and Holland coach Guus Hiddink spurned the chance to take over at Parkhead. Hiddink's adviser, Rob Jansen, said at the time: 'Yes, it is true, I don't think there will be a deal between my client and Celtic. I cannot say what the reason is – it is impossible for me to give any more comment at this time.'

Hiddink's decision not to go for the role left O'Neill as the prime candidate, though there was a huge amount of speculation linking Republic of Ireland manager Mick McCarthy to the role. O'Neill had a clause in his Leicester contract that allowed him to talk to interested clubs in the close season, ensuring he dominated the column inches both in the Midlands and north of the border. While O'Neill had worked wonders at Leicester, the chance to manage a club with attendances regularly pushing 60,000, Champions League football and a transfer kitty that would dwarf the Filbert Street coffers, a deal looked inevitable. O'Neill began to court the attention as he told the *Daily Mail* in late May: 'Anyone would be interested in a club like them. Celtic are absolutely massive, one of the biggest clubs in Europe and would interest most managers.'

In spite of this, however, Leicester remained surprisingly confident that they could hang on to the Ulsterman. Then chairman Sir Rodney Walker commented: 'There has been no formal approach by Celtic to Leicester. I am very relaxed despite this speculation, which doesn't surprise us. We don't believe this is a job in any case in which Martin would be interested.'

Talk of compensation pushing the £1 million mark would have helped cushion the blow at Filbert Street and eulogies already had begun coming in from Foxes favourites. Matt Elliot, brought to the club by O'Neill, hailed his impact at the club, but admitted no one would begrudge him a move to a bigger club. He told *The Sun*: 'I think it's fair to say Celtic would be getting one of the best managers around if they got Martin O'Neill. His motivational powers are what stand out more than anything; he seems to get the best out of his players, which is not always easy to achieve.'

Another player who flourished under O'Neill, Muzzy Izzet, added: 'Martin has done a great job with the resources he has had – and he has won things. It would be disastrous if he left Leicester. If you look at the starting XI just about every player has been brought in by Martin. I am sure there would be quite a few unhappy players if they let him go.'

Being a highly sought-after manager, one of O'Neill's strengths was his ability to carry on winning while boardroom battles raged around him, and there certainly was one going on here. Celtic had been looking for a manager for three months and needed to give their new boss as much time as possible with the players before the start of a crucial year – another season without success at Parkhead would not be tolerated.

With speculation rife, comment from the footballing world was never far away and an insight into O'Neill's character was given by a former Forest team-mate, Garry Birtles, who said: 'Perhaps Martin feels he has achieved everything he can at Leicester. Wherever he has gone in his career, he has always looked for that. I think he gets bored if he isn't constantly testing himself. Martin's outstanding quality is that he is single-minded. He knows exactly what he wants. It is inevitable he will eventually leave Leicester and that's not to be disrespectful to them – he is not a man to stand still.'

Meanwhile, at rudderless Parkhead, the players attempted to focus despite constant speculation as to who would lead them next term. Celtic favourite Paul Lambert told the *Leicester Mercury*: 'None of the boys have talked about the speculation. I think we have got bored of it. We have heard so much talk about whether it is going to be Guus Hiddink or Martin O'Neill. I don't think there will be much more talk until the guy actually walks through the door. It is important for the club to have somebody there to take them on to the next step and hope whoever it may be is going to be the right man for the job.' Kenny Dalglish would remain in temporary control until told otherwise, but temporary measures very seldom bode well at football clubs.

Not everyone thought a move to Scotland would benefit O'Neill. Former Celtic boss Lou Macari told the *Daily Record* in late May 2000: 'In Scotland, Celtic face just four challenges per season – when they play Rangers. But Martin thrives on being the underdog on a regular basis, taking Leicester to Liverpool and winning, getting a point at Arsenal and that sort of thing. Besides, Celtic's current squad is nowhere near enough. After turning down Leeds and Everton, I can't understand why Martin would want Celtic. OK, his management skills would be enough to close the gap on Rangers, and perhaps even overtake them, but Martin would find most domestic matches offered so little challenge that he might easily become bored. And if Celtic were to seize the crown, they would find themselves well short of the standard required in Europe, exactly the same as Rangers find on a regular basis.'

Macari's comments seemed to point towards a great challenge at Parkhead – a situation O'Neill relishes – and, within a few days, he had been offered the position. Despite late attempts from Leicester to persuade him otherwise, he agreed bumper terms in Glasgow. So the job of building a club razed to the ground during John Barnes' unsuccessful spell fell to Martin O'Neill.

On taking the job, O'Neill, who had idolised the Celtic players as a youngster, recalled how his father had told him that anyone should walk all the way to Parkhead if they had been offered a job there. The family ties to the club were underlined when Martin's brother Leo spoke out in the *Mirror*: 'We had all known for a few days that he was leaving Leicester for Celtic. It is sad that our parents could not be here for such a fantastic occasion, but the rest of us are absolutely overjoyed. There is a tradition of supporting Celtic in this village [Kilrea]. It's a huge job, but he will be up for it.'

Talk of a late hitch proved unfounded and in early June

2000 the move was finally confirmed. At his unveiling, O'Neill spoke of his pride at taking the job, saying: 'I presented myself and said I wanted the job and I didn't think there was much more to it than that. I didn't want them to interview another thirty-four candidates after that! But I am here now and am delighted. The league table doesn't lie; Rangers won by twenty-one points and there's an obvious gap to make up. I don't want to heap too much pressure on myself, but I want to make that up quickly. There is quality here at Celtic and I have to add to that.'

Speaking of joining his boyhood heroes, he added: 'I know it is easy to sit here on my first day and say that, but it was this football club and the 60,000 people who come here which was it. There is a chance for me to try and restore former glories.'

O'Neill spent the early part of the summer fulfilling obligations for the BBC at the European Championships in Holland and Belgium – with the usual transfer merry-go-round created by major tournaments. However, O'Neill insisted the pressure of European competition would not force him to drop his tried and tested policy. He said: 'I feel the top foreign players in the British game have been really good for the game. But there are a lot of mediocre foreign players preventing the young lads from coming through. This is something the club has to address. There are a huge number of mediocre foreign players out there. I was going to keep my eye on a couple of players who I could sign for Leicester, but the whole thing has now changed completely. The season starts at the end of July and the players are back at the end of this month. In terms of time, I will not get much, but that is part of the excitement.'

Meanwhile Celtic chief executive Alan MacDonald spoke of his delight at finally getting his man, also using the time to quell talk of Hiddink's supposed interest in the role. He said: 'When we met with Guus it was a visit that was widely reported, but numerous visits took place with a number of candidates. What we were trying to identify was people with experience, hunger and desire to do the job. We then decided as a board that Martin was the right man for the job. He is a manager of extreme high standing within the game and we are confident that his experience and knowledge will be invaluable in bringing success to Celtic. He has a reputation for building and developing successful sides; in addition as both a player and manager he has competed at the highest level in the English Premiership and had great experience of British football. It is that combination that convinced the board that Martin should become our manager. We identified four categories, top European coaches, European coaches that are aspiring to great success, top-quality British coaches and aspiring British coaches. The board wanted the best, so that took away two categories and once we did that you are down to small numbers and we finally narrowed it down to the man we have.'

O'Neill continued: 'I knew all about Celtic, of course, but the moment I arrived here to put pen to paper was when I realised how massive the club is. The attention in the media was quite exacting, but it was the second I was ushered out the door of the reception area to be greeted by hundreds of fans who had waited for four hours I really realised. I know they would have given a great reception to whoever had got the job, but these people had waited in the rain for hours to get a glimpse of the new manager. It is a special club.'

However with Kenny Dalglish still at the club in the role of director of football, O'Neill's position could have been interpreted as head coach, something he was keen to put straight. He continued: 'The board have given me a carte blanche to do what I see fit. I would love to be the football manager – that's what I want – I am old fashioned in that sense. I know I will be in charge of all football matters.'

Overturning Rangers' dominance in Scotland would not be an easy task and many preached patience for the Ulsterman, but any football fan knows it is never as simple as that. In a parting shot, then Leicester chairman told the *Irish Times*: 'I told Martin I thought he was making a wrong move, and that his career would be better served at Leicester – I am very disappointed. I spent one week trying to dissuade him from going and there were times when I thought he might change his mind. In the end, the pursuit of a personal dream related to his Roman Catholic heritage seems to have won the day.'

For any man, the chance to manage your boyhood club is the stuff of dreams, particularly for the tremendously proud Martin O'Neill, who recognised the pressure on his shoulders. He told the *Mirror*: 'Allan MacDonald shook my hand when I signed and said to me this was the most difficult job in football. After I vomited about three times, I thought to myself, he didn't tell me that in the interview. I realise how difficult this is going to be and I will want to enjoy it. It is a challenge. It is a massive gamble on my career, but I think football management is a massive gamble.'

While O'Neill's life to date seemed to have revolved around his tremendous talent at almost anything, he said planning rarely comes into his career choices; instead he relies on doors that open for him. He continued in the *Mirror*: 'I have never planned to be a manager, but this is one experience I did not want to miss. It's a fantastic opportunity for myself and is the chance to explore a dream. Despite all that has been written about my indecisiveness, it took me only two-and-a-half seconds to say yes to Celtic. If I was first choice or fifteenth choice it doesn't matter, but I genuinely believe I was one of the people the club were interested in all the time.'

Although a barren spell at Parkhead, compared with the embarrassment of riches across the city at Ibrox, had seen Celtic lose five managers in five years, O'Neill confessed this did not bother him. 'There have been eight managers here in the last nine years. By deduction I should get about seven-and-a-half months! I am pragmatic and I am not looking for 100 years, but at the end of it all you may realise the manager might need a little bit more time. I want to do it and at the same time I want to make up some ground. About the board giving me time, results and performances will determine how long I am here.'

O'Neill admitted many different factors had driven him, not least to try and emulate the great Jock Stein at Parkhead. He continued: 'I remember the Jock Stein side that won the European Cup in 1967 – that was unbelievable. It's been a massive club since those days and I feel there is a chance here for me to explore a dream.' However, he also admitted it had been a wrench to leave Leicester, saying that only the top job at Old Trafford would have been enough to take him away from Filbert Street. 'I couldn't get a result to save my life in the first dozen or so games at Leicester and it's fair to say the crowd were quite vociferous about that. Yet, after that, they had a big part to play in my staying as long as I did at the club. I had a fantastic rapport with the Leicester support and I would love to get something similar here at Celtic. People up here might think Leicester is not the be-all and end-all, but it has been part of my life. I loved working there and I appreciated it when they made a big effort to keep me. I hope it doesn't sound too sycophantic when I say that it was the lure of this football club more than anything that took me away from Leicester.'

The shadow of Brian Clough followed O'Neill wherever he went and, predictably, he was not short of a word to say when O'Neill was put in charge at Parkhead. Clough said he was with O'Neill the week before taking the big job, telling the *Mirror*: 'He still hadn't forgotten that, for all his remarkable success at Leicester, the fans were booing him soon after he arrived. He has got to look at himself now. At forty-eight, he is no spring chicken. I was only thirty-nine when I joined Leeds, the reigning league champions. Now I know I cocked that up by trying to push changes through too quickly, but at least I got a plum job before I was past it! After a time, the manager's brain cells start to pop and you just can't do it anymore, that will happen to Martin, too.'

Despite never being short of a cheap pop, Clough admitted he did have admiration for his former protégé. He continued: 'He knows the outside world, he can talk the players' language while keeping the media sweet. His football talent is known to all and, after working with me for five years, he has obviously learned something about management. Martin has served his time with smaller clubs and he knew he couldn't go much further with Leicester because they just weren't big enough. Celtic are one of the biggest in Europe. He will get a lot of brass for players and if he can beat Rangers to the title, he will be a Messiah – the new Jock Stein.'

Enjoying the newfound freedom of big bucks in the transfer market, O'Neill's first act as Celtic manager was to bring in forward Chris Sutton for a Scottish record fee, landing the Chelsea striker for around £6.5 million. Shortly after, he raided former club Leicester City for midfielder Neil Lennon. After years of upheaval at Parkhead, supporters, players and staff alike were calling for stability and were praying the Ulsterman could deliver. O'Neill is not the kind of man to go on a charm offensive, but he is honest enough to praise a rival when the moment is right. Ahead of the new season, he admitted Rangers were at an advantage, telling the *Daily Mail*: 'People who do well, regardless of which club they come from, get my admiration. I am not trying to win votes from fans across the River Clyde from Celtic Park. Believe me, I know what I will get when I go to Ibrox for the first time. But Rangers are the benchmark and I believe respect for the opposition will give my players additional determination to beat them. I am not trying to soften attitudes between Old Firm fans. For example, I understand that it's customary for the managers of both clubs not to go to games at Celtic Park or Ibrox if their teams aren't playing there. I won't break with that tradition if it helps avoid unpleasantness. What I am concerned about is doing the kind of job that guarantees I don't get abuse from the Celtic fans. But we can't deny that Rangers are a mile in front of us at the moment and that's where we will be starting from in the new season.'

O'Neill's first game in charge of Celtic was against minnows Bray Wanderers in a pre-season friendly. A hat-trick from Tommy Johnson gave O'Neill's side a 3-2 win – the first of many wins to come for the Ulsterman. Much of O'Neill's success had come from his insistence on doing things his own way. Kenny Dalglish had left the Hoops in a bitter wrangle and it seemed some of the squad would go the same way as O'Neill worked hard to stamp his authority on the under-performing club. He outlined his thoughts on his new club to the *Mail on Sunday*: 'Good players fit into systems I want rather than me building a team round an individual player. I will have a look at the overall pattern and see what is best. Anyone who has been on the pre-season tour can see for sure we need strengthening and my aim is to get three or four in very quickly. I have players in mind and work is going on behind the scenes to get them, but it doesn't happen overnight. I am not going into the specifics of what we need, but eventually the good players in the squad will be delighted that I am going to make a few quality signings to encourage them and give them a chance to challenge Rangers – that is what it is all about.'

Further friendly matches against Bordeaux and West Ham followed, giving O'Neill more time to assess the players before the start of the new season. However, with Scottish football starting earlier than south of the border, there was less time for him to adapt. He told the *Mirror*: 'I am getting to know the players every single day, but the time I will really know about them is when they are on the field of play in a competitive game. We have played a couple of friendlies, but that just helps the players get fit. There are some players, like Henrik Larsson, who I know very well indeed, but there are others I know less about and they may pleasantly surprise you under match conditions. Hopefully the team that I pick against Dundee United for the first game of the season will be ready to go and raring for it. I cannot believe the new season is nearly upon us, it seems like only ten minutes since Euro 2000 ended. It's getting close now, the excitement is mounting.'

In truth, it had been far from a dream pre-season for Celtic under their new boss, but O'Neill insisted friendlies were all about fitness and getting to know the squad. Defensive problems were finally addressed with the signing of Joos Valgaeren and O'Neill spoke of his delight at getting a player he had tracked for much of the summer.

O'Neill's first competitive match in charge of the Hoops was an away trip to Dundee United and it was a dream start for the him – with three points and a goal for new signing Chris Sutton. O'Neill had shaped a Celtic side that matched his mould of what a good side should have. Two strong, prolific strikers, in Henrik Larsson and Sutton, quality in the midfield, with Stilian Petrov and typical British steel in Paul Lambert and Alan Stubbs. It was a formula that would reap big rewards for Celtic that term.

Throughout the first few rounds of the Scottish league season, Celtic picked up scrappy wins as the side came to terms with how to work under their new boss, but nevertheless, they were winning. A 4-0 demolition of Luxembourg minnows Jeunesse Esch represented O'Neill's first big win in charge but he accepted a thorough overhaul of the club would be needed in order to bring prolonged success. He told the *Morning Herald*: 'We have to look at the domestic scene first and gain some strength from that, but a run in Europe would nourish us domestically. What I would like to see is us doing it on both fronts. Rangers have a squad capable of carrying a campaign on two fronts. They have Champions League experience and I think we could learn from that in trying to have a squad big enough to carry it on two fronts.'

O'Neill had walked the boards of Europe before so knew the stage well and it is often said that European football can put too much stress on a club. Certainly Europe would not daunt O'Neill, with his experience as a player proving invaluable to a Celtic side starved of domestic and international success.

If solid but unconvincing wins were enough for the new manager, Hearts and Rangers in successive matches would prove just how tough the Scottish Premier League could be. O'Neill told *The Sun* of his delight at being able to scrape through results, but also said a few big wins would be coming from his side. 'I have been really pleased with the players; the attitude they have shown has been terrific. There is a resilience about them. We have been able to do enough to win the games, but I think there is a lot more to come. It takes time to get a spirit going, but I have often said to the players that the best way to get a dressing room spirit relatively quickly is to win matches. In that respect the start we have had has been good, there are some really good players in the dressing room.'

The end of August gave O'Neill his first taste of Old Firm action as Rangers crossed the River Clyde for a typically tempestuous game at Parkhead. Despite having only a few wins under his belt, O'Neill's reputation was such that fellow SPL managers had to look up and take notice – if Celtic could ever really be overlooked anyway. Motherwell manager Billy Davies told the *Daily Record* that O'Neill's qualities would soon rub off on his players. 'He is a man who shows great pride in what he does and you only have to look at the way he was jumping around after Celtic scored their goals. I expect that same passion and commitment will rub off on the players in the dressing room. I know we are only one game into the season, but already Celtic are a much different side this season and they look a hungrier team – and with the appointment of the new manager they will prove difficult to break down. O'Neil has brought in some quality players and will no doubt add to them in the coming weeks. There were a lot of good players at Celtic irrespective of what happened to them last season. I am envious of their money; they can spend £6 million at a time whereas I am looking along the lines of £50,000 or £100,000. That is why we will give Celtic the utmost respect, because of who they are and who they have got on their staff.'

But there is no doubt the Old Firm (Celtic against Rangers) represented O'Neill's biggest challenge, with Dick Advocaat's side also enjoying a flawless start to the campaign. Ahead of his first derby, Celtic's new manager told the *Daily Mail*: 'I am nervously excited and if I ever lose that then it will be time to think about another job. I was always the same as a player. I am looking forward to it and I feel we are in good shape after winning our early games, but if Rangers are the benchmark then we have to face up to that. Confidence plays a massive part and I am sure if we could win this one it would help us greatly. I know, of course, that if we lose some people will paint it as doom and gloom and if we win it they will be talking about us winning the championship.'

Talking of his boyhood love for the fixture, O'Neill told the *Daily Record*: 'My first real memories are from the early sixties, although I can't really remember a particular fixture. In those days they only played twice and we used to look forward to the New Year game for months on end. That was when Jock Stein really took over and Celtic went into these games with confidence. I have never been to a live Old Firm game, although in those early days as a schoolboy my parents would never have allowed me to get on a boat from Belfast and see the game.' With family ties still running deep, O'Neill admitted many of the clan would make the short hop across the Irish Sea to watch the match. He continued: 'I think there will be at least three boat loads leaving for the game on Sunday. I have family and extended family, but I now have extended, extended family, people who have been supporting Celtic for thirty-five years, but have never been to Parkhead in their life.'

While Rangers had certainly got used to the manager merry-go-round at their neighbour's place, it did keep them on their toes in the derby on account of not knowing which Celtic would turn up. Buoyed by a solid start to the season and brimming with confidence under the highly animated Martin O'Neill, Celtic breezed through the Old Firm clash, picking up a phenomenal 6-2 win with O'Neill's deadly duo of Chris Sutton and Henrik Larsson each bagging a brace. After the match a triumphant O'Neill said: 'We got off to a fantastic start, but there were plenty of uncomfortable moments. They were absolutely fantastic, even at 4-1 I was thinking there is a long way to go. They got back to 4-2 and I think the only time I ever really felt comfortable was when Sutton put the sixth in. There is no feeling of euphoria because a few of them have been here a couple of years and know not to get too carried away with anything. But at the end of all this Rangers are still the benchmark and are a top-class side. We couldn't have dreamed for a better start. We could play another 100 years and not get a start like that again. I would have settled for scoring in the last minute and winning the game 1-0 – but there won't be many 1-0 games down here.'

True to his word, Celtic shipped seven goals in two games against Raith and Hibernian before their UEFA Cup campaign continued against HJK Helsinki. O'Neill's side could do no wrong and recorded a comfortable 2-0 home win. Despite the rivalry, there was one trophy in Celtic's cabinet that could not be bettered by their Ibrox rivals – the European Cup. Celtic's incredible achievement under the great Jock Stein brought the added burden of history onto O'Neill's shoulders in European competition. While the UEFA Cup would not represent the same achievement, it would more than satisfy supporters starved of success. O'Neill told *The Times*: 'When I was at Nottingham Forest around 1972 or 1973 all everyone seemed to talk about was the side that were runners-up in the league in 1966/67 and FA Cup semi-finalists in the same season. Everyone lived on that until we went past it. When we won the league, I remember Clough saying: "I wonder if they will start to remember this team."'

Celtic's remarkable opening spell at the start of the 2000/01 season represented their second-best start to a league campaign in 112 years. Indeed the only manager to better O'Neill's start was Jock Stein, who managed to record twenty consecutive wins in the 1966/67 season. O'Neill had notched an incredible twelve wins in a row but the run came to an end on 28 September in the second leg of their clash with HJK Helsinki at Parkhead. The two-goal win in Finland had given the Bhoys a great chance of progression, but a surprisingly poor performance on home soil saw the Finns win the game, but not do enough to seal the tie. After seeing his unbeaten run, which lasted two months, finally end, O'Neill said: 'The fact the run has ended does not mean a jot to me, although I would have preferred a win. But if anyone had said to me at me at the start of the season that we would have been unbeaten up until now I would have taken it.'

In early October, not long after he took the reigns at Parkhead, a call from his native Northern Ireland gave O'Neill an opportunity to do a good deed for his hometown club. Derry City, racked with debt, made a request to the Celtic boss to bring a side across from the mainland in order to raise funds from ticket sales. Despite the international break, O'Neill was more than happy to comply. While Henrik Larsson, Stilian Petrov and others were unable to travel due to commitments with their respective countries, a strong Celtic second string turned out at a packed Brandywell to keep the bailiffs at bay for the time being. After the event, O'Neill commented: 'I hope that this is the resurrection of Derry City, the start of something new. Derry wanted and needed this game as soon as possible, and we did our best to get over there as soon as we could. We would have come with our international players had the game not come at the start of an international week, but Derry City's need was essential, and we wanted to help. Those who I have spoken to involved with Derry have told us that by coming here, we have given the club a lifeline. I am sure with the money they will get from it, they will be able to clear up some of their debts.'

The game turned out to be a reasonable run-out for Celtic, with the final whistle denying Brendan Devlin a famous late equaliser. More importantly, the hastily arranged fixture brought in somewhere in the region of £70,000 for the club. Derry director Jim Roddy told the

Daily Record of how close the club had come to extinction: 'Martin replied to our request by fax half an hour before a shareholders' meeting and it was a distinct possibility the club might have been wound down. Since we knew Celtic were coming over there have been door-to-door collections and funds raised in local bars and that's helped us a great deal.'

Back on home soil, the Celtic juggernaut kept on rolling as St Mirren, St Johnstone and Dunfermline were all put to the sword courtesy of slim victories. Celtic had opened up a twelve-point lead over Rangers, who, in contrast to their archrivals, had endured a torrid few months, including an embarrassing defeat at St Johnstone. Boss Dick Advocaat blasted his players after the loss, a sure sign that the pressure created by O'Neill's Celtic was being felt across the River Clyde. The Dutchman told the *Mirror*: 'I have got a team of bigheads – they think they are better than they are. I have got Scottish internationals and Dutch internationals and they were very poor. My players have no idea about football, they want to look good and I am sick of it. I have twelve players injured, but I am not Houdini – I cannot fix that.'

Meanwhile, in Europe, O'Neill's Celtic had been drawn against Bordeaux in the next round of the UEFA Cup and travelled to southwest France, on the Garonne River, for a crunch tie with *les Girondins* in late October. After edging past HJK Helsinki in the first round, Bordeaux, with an attack spearheaded by Christophe Dugarry and Portuguese hitman Pauleta, represented a step-up in class. Before the game O'Neill was forced to fend off speculation linking him with a move for the England job after Kevin Keegan's departure – such was the respect commanded by the Ulsterman.

It would be fair to say Scottish teams suffer from travel sickness on the continent, so a 1-1 draw represented a big result for Celtic. Jackie McNamara gushed: 'That was easily the best away performance in Europe since I have been at the club. In fact, it is one of the best performances full stop. Bordeaux are a quality side and to get a draw in France is a brilliant result. It was really hard work, but we closed them down well. The way things are going this season we feel good about every game and we will go into the next match confident. Of course, the league is the most important thing for us, but nobody at Celtic doesn't want a run in the UEFA Cup.'

European nights at Parkhead are the stuff of legend – Manchester United, Barcelona and Celtic have all been rocked by the green-and-white army baying for blood in the stands – but in Martin O'Neill's opening season in charge of Celtic, visiting teams seemed to enjoy more success in Glasgow. In the lead-up to the return clash with Bordeaux, Celtic had endured a draining 3-3 draw with Motherwell before a 5-2 rout against Hearts in the quarter-finals of the Scottish League Cup (although they needed extra-time to progress to the last four). A one-goal win over Kilmarnock ensured the Hoops went in to the UEFA Cup match with a weekend win under the belts. However, in the crunch game, on 11 November, Bordeaux recorded a 2-1 victory to send Celtic crashing out of the competition. After the game O'Neill told the *Daily Record*: 'I honestly thought, looking at the likes of Dugarry, that we had knocked the heart out of them. I thought we had overwhelmed them in terms of passion and skill. I know that in a couple of days' time people might forget what actually happened out there, but please don't come back to me and say that Bordeaux were simply biding their time like cool customers. We had them beaten – we just didn't manage to kill them off. I would have to say it's one of the most galling defeats I have ever suffered as a manager.'

So O'Neill's first European adventure in charge of Celtic may have ended in heartbreak, but the stoic Ulsterman was determined that the high hopes he had for his first season were not about to be felled at the first hurdle. Tough fixtures in the lead-up to the game, including a Scottish League Cup tie, had dented his side's chances of progression. 'It sounds like an excuse, but I am sure our preparation wasn't as good as Bordeaux's,' he continued in the *Daily Record*. 'They did not have to play extra-time in a League Cup tie last week, plus two league games. That is hardly an ideal situation to be in, especially when you consider the reputation of Scottish football lives or dies by results in Europe. The goal must be to get Scottish teams to go further in Europe and we all have to do our bit. The domestic competitions are still very important, but you would like to think there is another way of doing it.'

Getting knocked out of the UEFA Cup in only the second round hurt O'Neill, who first fell in love with Celtic thanks to European competition – that cup final win over Inter Milan in 1967. He recalled in *The Sun*: 'I was at boarding school. The dean got a black-and-white TV set up and all 200 boarders were gathered in one room. There was a fuzzy picture on the TV, but the dean slapped it and the picture stayed on from kick-off to the end. I don't know if it was divine intervention. You wouldn't have to walk too far into the corridors of the club to see it is steeped in tradition from that time. Jock Stein is a legend and when you look at what he achieved it is unlikely ever to be surpassed. The idea is to try and get our own piece of history, and that is what I would like to do.'

Celtic's exit had given their new manager food for thought, and the Ulsterman admitted that the thought of bringing in new faces was constantly at the back of his mind. He continued: 'It is my job to strengthen the squad and I monitor that on a regular basis – it is almost an hourly thought. You always have a thought about bringing in someone on loan but, in general, I would rather have somebody who wants to sign a permanent deal. That might not always materialise, but the truth is we need to strengthen the squad. I have been given a budget this season and I have some money to spend and I am going to spend it. I might as well spend it because you get no thanks for saving it.'

Scoring goals was certainly no problem, with Henrik Larsson on fire for Celtic, as shown when he netted a brace in a 6-1 demolition of Hearts on 18 November.

Eight days later, O'Neill was to set to experience his first taste of Rangers' Ibrox, a cauldron of noise, pressure and anger vented at the visiting Celtic players and staff. While the club's massive win at Parkhead had nourished the Hoops' supporters for the last few weeks, all was forgotten when the two archrivals kicked off their second encounter of the season at lunchtime on 26 November. If O'Neill could steer his side clear of defeat, he would equal Jock Stein's record start to the season – 16 matches unbeaten. However, ahead of the tie, O'Neill insisted any comparisons between himself and the great Jock were way off the mark, telling the *News of the World*: 'Jock Stein is a god. What he achieved at this club simply defies belief. Nobody has ever got anywhere close to what he did here. We can only do our very best to try and win the championship and, if we manage that, to go on and give it our best shot in Europe. I am delighted with the start we have made and just hope we can keep it going for a while yet. But the only way to better what Jock achieved here would be to win two European Cups. When I was at Nottingham Forest we actually managed to go forty-two games unbeaten at one stage, and I think I played in twenty-eight of them. I was second top goalscorer behind John Robertson, yet when I mentioned this to Mr Clough recently he said he didn't remember the run – let alone me!'

Despite holding a mighty lead over their bitter rivals, it was Rangers who grabbed the headlines with a thumping scoreline of their own – eventually settling for five in a convincing demolition of their neighbours. New signing Tore Andre Flo was among the scorers for Rangers, who spent big money to bring the Norwegian to Ibrox. Despite the crushing loss, O'Neill was fully aware Old Firm games can produce shock results that have little bearing on form. He told the *Daily Record*: 'I said, no I hoped, at the start of the season that it would be close and this showed that it will be. We came into the game with plenty of confidence and that got wounded today, but I always said that Rangers are a very strong side and there is no doubt about that. If you had said at the start of the season that we would be anywhere near Rangers at this stage I would have been delighted. Now if we go into the winter break a point ahead at the top that is fine.'

The Old Firm clash certainly acted as a reality check, serving as proof that the talented Rangers squad were not going to lay down and hand the title over to their bitter rivals. But the winter break would give O'Neill the opportunity to assess his squad and pick up on its shortcomings. He told the *Mirror*: 'Rangers are a very good team with a squad not only capable of competing in Scotland but of being of top quality should they play in the English Premiership. When I arrived here in July we had an awful lot of work to do to catch them and we still do. My players have been fantastic, although we deserved to get beaten because we did not do well enough on the day. At the start of the season I wanted to have a proper look at the full squad. Some of the players have done phenomenally well while others have surprised me. Even if we bring in reinforcements, the players already here are still capable of battling into the side. We have only dropped seven points so far because we have been so consistent, but even if we had come away from Ibrox unscathed I would still have said we need a stronger squad. We are not in a position where we can cope with losing five players through injury, and need to get more in.

I want us to be good enough to compete not just at domestic level but in Europe as well. The truth is we haven't got that strength in depth – but that doesn't mean we pack it in and say we can't do it. When we beat Rangers it gave us a lot of confidence and the most consistent side eventually wins the championship. The current Rangers squad is probably the strongest they have ever had. But I have not been let down by any of our players, I think we are a decent side – though far from the finished article. We have done really fine so far and there are going to be hiccups along the way.'

He believed that Celtic's strong start to the season failed to mask deeper issues within the club. He told the *Herald*: 'There is just no way that I could spend £12million on one player, which is what Rangers did last week. That is not something we could do here. I have to deal with a plc board and I don't know what Rangers have to do, except that they can go out and spend that kind of money. They buy a player who cannot play in the UEFA Cup because he has been cup-tied, and they do that to signal that they want to win the league championship. If David Murray and Dick Advocaat can do that then that is good for them – but it is not something I can look at. I don't want to go on and on about the same thing – but I did say when I arrived here that the squad needed strengthening. I think, if I can remember correctly, that Dick Advocaat suggested he had two teams available, one for the league and the other for Europe – and I think that is right when he has all his players available. We are two years behind them in development after the traumatic times the club had last season.'

A goalless draw with Hibernian may not have been the ideal way to bounce back from defeat, but consecutive wins against Dunfermline and Dundee kept Rangers at arm's length. One of the most protracted transfer sagas saw O'Neill finally snare fellow Celtic-mad Ulsterman Neil Lennon. The Leicester midfielder moved to Parkhead for a deal of around £5 million. Lennon had long been linked with a reunion with his former boss and O'Neill explained why he raided his former club. 'There were a number of clubs who enquired and put bids in for Neil when I was manager of Leicester,' he told the *Daily Star*. 'I told him about them and why I turned them down – I wanted him to stay and see things through. Sometimes you have to accept the fact that a player no longer wants to play for you. If these players want to leave for better things then there is not a lot really you can do about it. We were lucky that we were able to keep Neil and the other good players we had at Leicester motivated enough to stay and play for the football club. Neil actually came to Leicester in difficult circumstances and managed to play through them. He would have been very surprised to hear the fans baying for the blood of the manager who had just signed him only minutes into his first game. He had a good spell at Leicester, probably the best in the club's history – we reached three cup finals, winning two of them, and also qualified for Europe. When I asked and put an offer in during the summer, Leicester rejected that offer. I left it at that until Peter Taylor contacted me again – it was a big surprise to me. My interest waned a bit, but I didn't forget about him, even though it was Peter who initiated the move. He decided to sell for possibly two reasons, either Neil wasn't playing at the level he knew he could achieve, or, secondly, he didn't think Neil was as good a player as I thought he was. When I got the call I decided to follow it up and I put in an offer which was rejected, but I was doing what I thought was in the best interests of the football club. The whole transfer saga became a bit long-winded and a bit too public for my liking. Eventually the clubs agreed a fee, which was less than the bid I made in the summer, but these things happen in football. I think that Neil is worth every penny. He will do really well at his football club because, more than anything, he can play and he has a big heart.'

While O'Neill was never afraid of tinkering with his squad, it was clear he saw Celtic as a long-term project that would take time to get right. His dips into the transfer market were spread out, never panic buying, showing he developed strategy to improve the side while keeping faith with those who were already performing well at Parkhead. He told the *Mirror*: 'I have said before that I have been pleased with the efforts of the new boys but, other than the two lads signed on the same day, they have been signed intermittently. It was obvious that we needed a few strong defenders and Joos came in just a week before the start of the season and I have been very, very pleased with him...Neil Lennon has just played one game, Ramon Vega has not even kicked a ball for us. But it has been the attitude of the players who were already here that I have been delighted with. I don't think that there is a fear element among the players that were already here; they know that if they are doing well enough, not only will I want them here short term, but if they are young enough and good enough we want them here a bit longer. It is not a matter of me getting in my own people. I have never worried about that, you just have to accept that at a football club. At the clubs I have been at before people have been there when I arrived and they were still there when I left. If the boys that have come in can mix with the group that are already there, then I am delighted with that. It is not a matter of me changing it around here, I just think we need some players in.'

A 6-0 demolition of Aberdeen in mid-December, thanks largely to a Henrik Larsson hat-trick, saw Celtic return to their devastating best. Comfortable wins over St Mirren and Dundee ensured O'Neill's side went into the New Year brimming with confidence – cemented with a 6-0 rout over Kilmarnock in their first fixture of 2001. The Scottish winter break, throughout most of January, would give O'Neill a chance to take stock of a blistering first term in charge of the Hoops, and widespread opinion was that he had worked wonders with a squad that, only the previous season, had been low on confidence, form and quality. Ever the realist, O'Neill admitted he was all too aware that a time would come when the Celtic bubble would burst and the criticism he had largely managed to avoid would find him. He told *The Sun*: 'It might not be this season or next, but it will happen to me – it is inevitable and is part of the job. I have been surprised by the ferocity of it all, though. Dick Advocaat has been under pressure this season for what could only be termed a couple of lapses.'

Speaking of his first six months at the helm of Celtic, he continued: 'I always wanted to take a risk; I want to win something here to prove something to myself. I was aware of the risks of Celtic, but this was the job I wanted to go for. It might still go horribly wrong. I got a taste of that last year when I came up to watch the game against Lyon in the UEFA Cup. It was two weeks after Henrik Larsson broke his leg and there was despondency around the place. I realise I have had a relatively long honeymoon period, but I have been too long in the game to dwell on that. It was nice to hear people say I would get time and that Celtic needed stability, but I did not believe I would get the time. More so than ever before that is not the nature of this game. I knew I had to get things up and running pretty quickly. Now we have only dropped nine points and there is no way I can be displeased. I am not in a comfort zone, but little has been there to make me moan. The attitude of the players who were already here – let alone the ones who have signed – has been excellent. We have achieved nothing yet and even though it has gone well, life could have been the opposite and I would still have wanted this. It has been a really long year, though, I have never known one more frantic.'

O'Neill added: 'If you are going to win something you must have a strong mentality. It is a fine balancing act. I saw matches from last season on video that told me we needed more strength. I knew some of the players and, tape by tape, they became more familiar – if you see a pattern emerge then it is more easy to solve. Yet I never wanted to prevent people from playing and the fact we have scored sixty goals in the league suggests we want to attack. The difference between the start of the season and now is that there is belief about the team – even after we lost to Rangers. The team has confidence in each other; they feel their team-mates will help them. I am pretty poor at switching off. I will keep tabs on English football when I stop because, do you know what? The truth is I am one sad individual.'

A trip to Hearts in early February, courtesy of a majestic Henrik Larsson hat-trick, kept Celtic well clear of the competition and sent out an imposing message to Rangers and the chasing pack. Buoyed by the win, O'Neill believed his players were stronger than last year. He told *The Sun*: 'The players were disappointed the previous year. They lost by 21 points and felt they had given up the ghost. It wasn't a case of imposing myself on them – they knew what they had to do. I hate the phrase: "Look at yourself in the mirror," because I am so ugly, but perhaps that is what they had to do. You don't lost the league by that number of points and think you're unlucky.' But O'Neill admitted the league was his top priority, Celtic's bread and butter and domestic dominance was the first mountain the Bhoys needed to climb. If O'Neill's squad did have any doubts over their Championship credentials, they were firmly put to rest in the Old Firm clash just days after dispatching Hearts so convincingly. While the scoreline may not have been so emphatic, with a solitary Alan Thompson goal settling the match, the impact it had on the season was massive. Pulling further away from their bitter rivals, it appeared Celtic were cantering towards the title. The

Celtic fans were chanting: 'We're gonna win the league' but, at least publicly, O'Neill preached caution. 'The boys are aware this was a big win and it definitely gives us a cushion,' he told the *Daily Mail*. He was aware there could be plenty of mistakes before the end of the season, but it was a massive win.

As if to support his theory, a surprise 2-2 draw with Dunfermline in the fourth round of the Scottish Cup had the critics calling burnout at Parkhead. O'Neill, meanwhile, maintained his stance by claiming he needed a bigger squad in order to compete on all fronts. 'We are a big enough club to try to get extra players in,' he told the *Mirror*. 'If you ask any major manager they will tell you the same thing. For example, Alex Ferguson has been able to swap some of his players, leave a few out and allow others to have a short break. I am not in a position to do that yet, nor have we won anything, but it comes with a bit of success and a bit of experience. Liverpool are like that now. I spoke with Ron Yates, their chief scout, at the beginning of the season and he said Liverpool now have an extra player for each position for the first time for a number of seasons. They have four strikers and if you compare that to ourselves with two lads who are generally the pivotal point and, naturally, I would be concerned if anything happened to them. That is why we need to keep developing if we want to be some sort of force in Europe. But that is next season.'

A 1-0 win over Motherwell, which was met by a wall of near silence at Parkhead, urged the Celtic boss into a passionate plea to the club's supporters. He said: 'Perhaps

I got spoilt by the Old Firm atmosphere and I must admit I have never experienced anything like that noise level in my time in football. But I expected more noise from minute one against Motherwell. Sometimes this team entertains and gets the crowd going, but other times the crowd need to get the team going. I know the fans can get a bit frustrated, but I honestly don't think this season that they have had too much to get frustrated about. We all have to pull together, because winning things is still the most difficult thing to do. We still haven't dropped a point at Celtic Park and even against Motherwell I don't think we played poorly.'

The passion of football fanatics was tarnished in the coming weeks though, when Celtic's Northern Ireland midfielder Neil Lennon was singled out for sectarian abuse while on international duty. Rangers supporters have typically favoured the Unionist population of Northern Ireland and Lennon's decision to move to Celtic clearly angered a senseless minority in his home country. The £6 million player, signed by fellow Ulsterman O'Neill just months before, received death threats from suspected Loyalist thugs and was placed under police protection. When Northern Ireland faced Norway in a friendly at Windsor Park, Lennon spoke of his disappointment at the vitriol that had been aimed his way, saying: 'I cannot understand it because I am just here to play for my country. It is a privilege to be asked to play for Northern Ireland and I want to do that to the best of my ability.'

The incidents sparked nationwide disapproval, with Ulster Unionist minister Michael Gimpsey having his say.

'That anyone should issue threats to one of Northern Ireland's players simply because he has signed for a particular team in the Scottish Premier League is appalling. Let no one be in any doubt that this type of thuggery has absolutely no place in sport and that to fail to condemn it is to fail to support our national team. We don't need, or do we want, this sort of behaviour, especially at a time when the entire football family is pulling together for the future well-being of the game.'

Lennon admitted that the bitter incident had caused him to rethink his international career. He continued: 'I hope to be back to play for Northern Ireland again, but I will have to go back to Scotland to discuss the situation with my family and Celtic manager Martin O'Neill. I knew there would be a minority who would have a go at me, but I want to thank those who got behind me.'

At Parkhead, friends rallied around the Ulsterman, including O'Neill. The Celtic manager told *The Sun*: 'You go over there and you want to take pleasure and enjoyment out of playing for Northern Ireland. If you go over and play poorly and get booed by the crowd then that is part of the game. But if you are going to take a constant barrage simply because of who you play for it is very disappointing. [Lennon is] someone who has always wanted to play for his nation [and] is being booed by his fellow countrymen. It has been a big concern for him. It is alright to say he should be able to deal with it, but this is pretty traumatic. He is twenty-nine and he has clouds hanging over him when he plays international football, which he really wants to do. Seriously, Neil feels this is a situation he can't win from.'

Speaking on whether Lennon should continue to represent his country, O'Neill added: 'If he does go then he might not get a single ounce of enjoyment from it even if Northern Ireland win. It is a situation he should not find himself in. I have total sympathy right now and I am concerned. He needs to be able to go and enjoy it. You cannot do that if your own crowd are giving you stick – and it has nothing to do with what you are doing on the field. I want him to take his time to think about this and I really hope it doesn't affect his club form. I thought it would have gone past this stage; that they would like him no matter who he played for if he gave his all. It seems strange that this should have been taken on board. Does this mean he shouldn't have signed for Celtic? Maybe we were naïve, but we hadn't thought about that happening when we spoke about him signing here. Now he is worrying about his family and all the other issues...The concern came when you saw the graffiti, and he went through a very uneasy seventy-two hours in Belfast.'

Despite this, just a matter of weeks later, Lennon announced his decision to continue playing for his country. After hearing the decision, O'Neill said: 'Neil obviously consulted his family and made that decision, so I am pleased he has made his decision and I am glad he has done what he has done at this minute and we will see how it goes. I am not too worried about what sort of message it may or may not send out. If it's his real decision that he wants to continue then I totally abide by that.' The Celtic boss had spoken of his fears that Lennon's focus might be taken off his club, but was relieved to find it hadn't. He continued: 'It hasn't shown in his play, which I am really pleased about. I think he has coped very, very well indeed. I am more pleased that he has made the decision now rather than letting it drift on and on and the decision then might have played on his mind. Now I think he can get on with things, although I don't honestly think it was affecting his play for Celtic.'

Lennon himself concluded: 'The decision I have made was not taken lightly as I felt it was important to consider the feelings of my family and friends as they have been through a very traumatic experience. Obviously I hope that they and myself do not have to suffer under these circumstances again. I am proud to be a Celtic player and I am enjoying my time at the club very much. I hope that in the future I will be given the opportunity, as a Celtic player, to also enjoy my international career.'

O'Neill told the *Glasgow Evening Times*: 'My role was really very minor – my thoughts were he should give it another go. I wasn't there when it happened, therefore I didn't get the whole feel of it all. But I thought that perhaps with the next game being a World Cup qualifier, maybe the crowd would get behind all of the team. Neil thought himself that it was all a wee bit of a distraction for the rest of the players, and I think that was a concern as much as anything. He has now made the decision and I would hope the crowd would get behind him for the team as much as anything else. If he doesn't play well, he would expect the normal amount of criticism but, hopefully, it would be before he has actually misplaced any passes. His performances for us have been top class, before and after the event. I knew that the longer the deliberations went on it might start playing on his mind a bit. But I never had any real concerns about it affecting his club form. I am pleased he has made the decision and that it hasn't hung around – he is going to go for it and we will see how it goes.'

O'Neill's decision to back his star midfielder had not been a difficult one. Any manager would protect one of their squad, but, for the Ulsterman, his backing went beyond a normal manager's loyalty to his player. O'Neill had a personal understanding of sectarian tensions in Northern Ireland.

O'Neill admitted going into March still competing on multiple fronts was a welcome change from his experiences in England. While Leicester had achieved solid finishes in the Premier League, their main chance of silverware generally finished with the League Cup in February. He told the *Mail*: 'We all have to keep going until the very end – the players, myself and everyone else at the club. This is a new thing for me. At Leicester I would maybe have the Worthington Cup final to look forward to in February or March, but after that it was simply a case of trying to win as many games as we could to finish as high up the league table as possible. The chairman wouldn't let us stop going anyway and would remind me of the extra money involved the higher you finished. But this could well end up being the longest league run-in in history between the weather and the problems over foot and mouth. Whatever happens, we will be ready for it.'

While Celtic secured victories over Dunfermline and St

Johnstone to maintain their place at the top of the table (and also beat Hearts in the quarter-finals of the Scottish Cup), Rangers huffed and puffed in second place waiting for a slip-up across the River Clyde. Sadly for Dick Advocaat, O'Neill was desperate to ensure his charges were not about to take their foot off the gas at such a crucial point of the season.

League Cup success was something Martin O'Neill had become accustomed to. So far in his short Celtic career, beating Rangers had become his forte so when Celtic met their bitter rivals in the semi-finals of the competition, sparks were sure to fly. Hampden Park played host to the early anticipated clash. Sure enough three players were sent off, two for Dick Advocaat's side, but it was Celtic who progressed. Chris Sutton had put Celtic in front with an early goal which was swiftly doubled by Henrik Larsson. Jorg Albertz hauled Rangers back into the match but a second from the irrepressible Larsson sent the Hoops through. It was another bad-tempered clash between the country's top two. Certainly there had been plenty of bad blood between Rangers and Celtic in the lead up to the tie and both manager's had attempted to diffuse simmering tensions in Glasgow.

The end of March brought with it the League Cup final and O'Neill's first chance at silverware. He was aware that, as was the case south of the border, the League Cup does not enjoy the same status as the league or FA Cup, but having tasted success at Leicester, he was not about to devalue the competition completely. 'People have described it just as some in the south did with the

Worthington Cup,' he said, 'but I have never done that, although I can understand the need to prioritise the way Manchester United have felt in the past when in the Champions League as well as other competitions. But I remember that when Arsenal and Chelsea met in the semi-final they had supposedly been uninterested in the tournament, yet both played their best teams. It was the same when we met Rangers in the last round here. I am sure Liverpool are happy they won the Worthington Cup and I certainly was when Leicester did. But I want to win this trophy and get my first with Celtic.' Only Kilmarnock stood in the way of Celtic, but the showpiece event at Hamden Park proved a one-sided affair as the Hoops eased to a 3-0 victory, with Henrik Larsson netting a hat-trick.

Not that the win meant O'Neill and his Celtic players could rest on their laurels: 'I can recall speaking to Walter when I was at Leicester and I was in the process of joining Celtic,' said the triumphant manager. 'He told me that, no matter what happens in Glasgow, no matter what you win, there is no comfort zone. That was good advice. So, although it is a great pleasure for everyone connected with the club to have this trophy, nothing is being taken for granted. It is just one victory and one cup and we all know we will have to continue to work very hard. As far as I am concerned, we must get on with the business. We will enjoy ourselves – of course we will – but we must focus upon the other prizes on offer this season and in the future. It is premature for anyone to state that I have been a success. When I look at the history of this club and think of the achievements of the late Jock Stein and others, then it would be foolish to claim anything.'

He continued: 'There is nowhere else I would fancy going to be perfectly honest. This club has absolutely everything. To be involved in decent days of European football again, that's what a manager wants. I don't want to get carried away with myself, far from it. We have a championship to win and the possibility as well of trying to get another Hampden final in the Scottish Cup. But European football is tangible, it's still the ultimate and, if you were having some really decent days in European football over the next couple of seasons, that is all you can ask for. With the crowd behind you – and when the Celtic crowd is behind you, it is certainly behind you – it is something to behold.'

While Europe may have been the final frontier for O'Neill, he insisted he would wield whatever transfer funds were given to him sensibly. He continued: 'I don't think the fans will be too worried about this and I am not too worried about it either. So whatever money is available for me I will go for it and I will spend it. Whether it is large or small it doesn't matter. I know in my mind what will be needed to try and be half-decent in European football, but some of the big sides in Europe, like Juventus and Barcelona, have fallen by the wayside this season, so it has been difficult. I think you need a number of years to get there and Manchester United didn't succeed at the first time of asking. It would be great for us to win the league and, if we did that, we would have only one qualifying game, but we might be drawn against a seeded team like Juventus.'

As the season moved into its penultimate month, few

doubted Celtic's ability to win the title as O'Neill's side swept past Aberdeen and Dundee in quick succession. It seemed only a matter of time before the SPL trophy would return to Celtic Park, and victory over St Mirren at Celtic Park on 7 April secured Celtic only their second league title in twelve years. A 2-1 victory, while not the emphatic result many had expected, was enough to win the title for Celtic, the thirty-seventh in their history and the quickest title win in twenty-six years (with five games of the season remaining). Following the result, O'Neill was adamant this was one of the greatest days of his decorated football career. He said: 'It has been a phenomenal day, it's as good a day as I have had in football. I was lucky to have a few decent ones as a player – and some really bad ones as well – and some decent days as a manager with Wycombe and Leicester. This is special – we have won a championship. As my old mentor Brian Clough used to say, the team that wins the championship has usually been the best over the season. It was as pleasing a moment as I could imagine. It feels as though it has been the longest season of my life – at other times if feels as though it is only five minutes ago that we kicked off against Dundee United. Since the break I thought that there were a couple of significant matches. The Hearts game, where we won 3-0, was one and the win against Motherwell, when Lubo Moravcik scored a late goal, was another. I didn't want to drop points that night and give anybody hope who was chasing us at the time. We deserved this, we have won twenty-eight out of thirty-three league games and I don't imagine we will ever do that again.'

Neil Lennon spoke of his immense pride at winning the title, telling the *Sunday Express*: 'It is hard to put it all into words. I never dreamed I would see this day when I started the season at Leicester City because, to be honest, I thought my chance of joining Celtic had gone. But I will never forget this. I might never win another championship, but no one can take this away from me. Hopefully we will do the treble and then go on and do well in the Champions League. And we can certainly go forward with confidence because the spirit here, moulded by Martin O'Neill in the same way he did at Leicester, is unbreakable.'

Five league games still remained, including an Old Firm derby, and O'Neill admitted it gave him the chance to rest some players and blood youngsters. 'Rangers will be roaring back with a bit of venom. Could you tell David Murray not to produce any more money? I am still of the belief that they have a lot of talented footballers. I wouldn't go to Ibrox with a youth team, but I will give some of the younger lads a chance to show what they can do. Some of the boys have been very strong and would deal with European football with no problem, but I haven't got enough of them.'

While Celtic's remaining league games were little more than a formality, the FA Cup semi final with Dundee United in mid-April represented a serious challenge for O'Neill and his all-conquering side. Two goals from Henrik Larsson, enjoying an incredible season with the Bhoys, helped Celtic on their way to a 3-1 victory to leave them one game away from an historic treble. The following league game against Hearts, which had been moved to a 6pm kick-off on Sunday to accommodate Sky television, irked O'Neill, who was adamant his side should have lifted the trophy the day they won the trophy. He said: 'It seemed strange to me at the time and now the wisdom of it is even more questionable. I could have understood it had there been two or three sides vying for the title on the same day, but Celtic Park was the only place it could end up. It does give us another chance to celebrate, but I would be disappointed if the late kick-off meant some of our fans were unable to stay for the party. Our Irish supporters are the ones that always spring to mind in these situations, but the fact is that anyone living outside Glasgow will find they will be getting home late. Rules are rules and we have to abide by them, but it is far from ideal. I just hope most people will hang around. It will be a lovely occasion for everyone.' A one-goal victory over Hearts ensured the Celtic Park faithful had plenty to cheer about, with the giant SPL trophy paraded in front of a packed house and the irrepressible Celtic manager leading the celebrations.

The Scottish Cup final was just weeks away, but a trip to Ibrox still awaited the jubilant Celtic players. O'Neill sent a predictably strong side across the River Clyde, with Henrik Larsson, Lubo Moravcik and Neil Lennon all in the starting line-up. Despite having the league trophy safely locked away, defeat at the Old Firm would not be tolerated and a 3-0 win at Ibrox rubbed salt into the gaping wounds of Dick Advocaat's beaten side. The win was Celtic's first at Ibrox in six years. Humble in victory, O'Neill opted to play down the significance of the win, saying: 'I know Rangers will come roaring back. I expect a big reaction from them, they are a powerful outfit.'

The party continued at Celtic but, perhaps understandably, league results slipped as Dundee and Kilmarnock picked up surprise wins over the champions. However, just weeks before the final Celtic had hammered cup final opponents Hibernian 5-2 in a dress rehearsal for the showpiece event.

To the surprise of no one, O'Neill was rewarded with the Manager of the Year award for masterminding the miraculous turnaround at Parkhead. After collecting the award, he commented: 'I am naturally very, very pleased. If somebody said that we would take fifty-two points out of fofty-seven at home this season I would gladly have accepted that. That comes down to the efforts of the players and I am absolutely thrilled. I might have a couple of glasses of wine to celebrate.'

Defeat to Kilmarnock in the final league game of the season ruined Hearts' hopes of European football and O'Neill's decision to drop nine first-team regulars did not sit well with some opponents. Hearts striker Stéphane Adam told *The Sun*: 'I have been in football for fifteen years and I have never known anything like this. To put out a reserve team when others were still trying to qualify for Europe shows a total lack of respect. I am very disappointed with Celtic's attitude.' But O'Neill hit back, claiming it was his decision and his decision alone who played for Celtic. He said: 'It is my prerogative as manager of Celtic to decide who I play. It is a thirty-eight-game season and I have to be responsible for Celtic Football Club. We have a cup final to look forward to and I am sure every other side would have done the same thing. Who is to say that if I had played all the full players they would not have had one eye on the cup final itself?'

There was an air of inevitability around the cup final as Celtic ran riot over Hibernian, eventually settling for a 3-0 win to confirm their total dominance of Scottish football. Supporters, players and the media were gushing in their praise of Martin O'Neill and the way he had turned around a battered and bruised Celtic side. Before the match, O'Neill had expressed some concerns about the pitch at the Scottish national stadium, but this did not hamper his rampant players. Speaking of his startling success, O'Neill told *Scotland on Sunday*: 'We had some very good players here, who responded brilliantly, and when I brought a couple of boys in we started to win a few matches and that created a good spirit. When we started to win in a bit of style, the good players gained confidence in themselves and each other. Not in my wildest dreams did I think we could achieve what we have this season; there is a lot of work still to be done, but we have been very strong this season.'

While domestically it would be impossible to better the 2000/01 season, O'Neill had been campaigning all year to improve on the European stage, and although qualification for the Champions League may have represented a step up in class, it was also a tournament in which O'Neill was desperate to compete. 'I took a gulp of air when I looked at the teams we could be playing against,' he continued. 'The

149

aim is to try and progress as quickly as we can. Initially it was about restoring our pride domestically. Now, having done that, we must keep it going and attempt to make inroads into European football. Whether that will take a year or three years, I don't know. If we had not won the league this year, our fans would have been saying this summer: "Right, you have had a year to bed in, now you have got to go for it." So the expectations won't be a whole lot different this season. At least that is what I console myself with in moments of despair.'

Given what the club had gone through before O'Neill's arrival at the club, the 2000/01 season would go down as the stuff of legend at Celtic Park. Certainly it had been hoped the popular, enigmatic Irishman would be a hit with the fans, but few could have predicted the instant dominance the Ulsterman was able to instil at Celtic. O'Neill took them from floundering, fractured and under-achieving to the dominant force in Scotland. Next season would bring with it the potential to rub shoulders with Europe's elite, giving O'Neill the chance to negotiate a path to the European Cup final, treading the same boards he had done as a Nottingham Forest player.

'I was asked about targets when I came here and all I wanted to do was try to restore some confidence in the dressing room,' he said. 'The confidence took a battering because Rangers were so strong in the previous year. But they made a dodgy start to the season and we strung a number of wins together. My first aim was to get to know each other and certain players have actually responded brilliantly and continued to play well throughout the course of the season. We started winning matches and there was a good spirit in the dressing room, which was important. I don't know what I would have settled for, but what I set out to do was to restore confidence and close the gap on Rangers by winning a couple of games. This is an immense club – I know you might say that playing here with 60,000 people is a paradox, but still it is a great, great club and this is immensely satisfying. When we reflect on this we will say, "Yeah, that's fantastic", but European football has got to be the ultimate aim for a football club of this size and history. Our opening game in Europe is going to be hard enough. The second phase of the Champions League: well, that's the ultimate, where everybody is trying to be. Playing football is the biggest buzz of all; I don't care what anyone says. This is a sideshow by comparison. It's a different feeling, as John Robertson has explained to me many times. You get a reflected glory from your team. But if you said to me years ago, "You will be playing European Cup finals, like Di Stefano and Puskas and other immortals did," I would have taken that. As time goes on you can no longer play, but this is the second best thing.'

A major coup for O'Neill in shaping his Celtic squad was agreeing a new contract for Henrik Larsson, who had run riot in the SPL, scoring over fifty goals for the Bhoys and turning out match-winning performances for his manager. Speaking of his star player, O'Neill told *The Sun*: 'A lot of players in his position might not have stayed. He is in the minority of players who would think the way he did – but that is not to say he is the only one. Neil Lennon came up here and even though he is well paid, showed he wanted to put the football first. Yes, I was delighted Henrik stayed and I told him that when I shook his hand – I always felt he would stay. I knew his heart was with this club and that was a big factor. It showed when he still produced amazing football when I don't feel he was being paid what he was worth. Perhaps others were on more money and not doing what he did – and only now do I feel he is getting his rewards for what he has done for us. It would have been a huge disappointment for the players and fans if a player of his calibre had left Celtic, but now I believe he can have the same sort of season next year as he has just had.'

O'Neill admitted that while the 2000/01 season had been incredible, it would mean little when the new season kicked off in July. He continued: 'People keep asking me how do we follow last season's success? We are a bit ahead of ourselves, admittedly, but there would have been that pressure anyway, whether we were successful last season or not. To be honest, it could go down to the wire – it could be that close. Fans always expect success at a big club like Celtic, but what we achieved last season is in the past. It is gone. The trophies are a nice reminder of what we achieved, but we have to start again. The slate has been wiped clean and we must do it all over again. Expectations have been raised, but we are ready for the challenge. A year ago I was new to the job, I was new to a lot of the players. A lot of them probably felt they were on trial and they probably felt they had something to prove, but everyone is more settled now and that helps. Some people regard me as a saviour, but I am only doing my job.'

But management for O'Neill meant more than just coaching and he insisted on having a say in the running of his football club. Explaining his desire to be more than just a coach, he added: 'The manager's job has changed incredibly in the last twenty years. There is a feeling these days a manager should just manage the team, not the club. Most chief executives would want to consign the old way to the past. Leicester attempted to introduce the new way, but I was vehemently opposed to it. I want to be involved in the running of the football club. I don't want to run everybody else's job, but I want an input. A football club of Celtic's size is so big I can't run around telling the chief executive what to do, but I expect to run this club in terms of footballers and in terms of their contracts and all the things younger managers are tending to shy away from. I will get sacked eventually if results go badly, so I want to be responsible as much as I can for the input into getting those results. I have learned to have the courage of my convictions. If you get something wrong, don't worry too much about it and try to keep the major mistakes to a minimum. That is why I have never phoned Brian Clough for advice. I tend to go with my gut feeling and if it is wrong then it is my mistake.

'I have had a really good year,' he continued, 'but I would have said that even if it had been mediocre. I know, though, that management is fickle and we are judged on the day – that will never change. What is special is the atmosphere created by 60,000 people who gather here every second weekend. It is almost like a sharing. So many people come up during the course of the week. They gather outside just to gaze at the club's doors, it is something very special to people. The moment when the lads go into a huddle and 60,000 make an unbelievable noise all around the ground – that is when you know it is all worthwhile. I know one day the 60,000 will be baying for my blood – I am sure in the course of time that will happen.' He went on to say that managers will come and go, as will the players, but the fans won't. 'When I came here, confidence was low, even among the good players. They had been mauled by Rangers and it was a matter of helping them get their confidence back. We lost Mark Viduka and brought in Chris Sutton and Joos Valgaeren, so, in effect, we had only one addition to the squad. But I was really pleased with their attitude going into the season. If they had wanted to down tools, there would not have been a place for them, but they all decided they wanted to return the club to some of its former glory. In terms of confidence, winning the first Old Firm game was fantastic, but then we realised the fans were saying "championship here we come". The defeat by Rangers in November brought our supporters back to reality, which is no bad thing. I have got a dodgy knee and I remember once it just caved in on me when I was jumping on the touchline. I was embarrassed, but didn't want to let people know I was in real pain. I am sure the blood pressure goes up and down during the course of a match. I would never want to be monitored and I am not one for going on a bike to keep in shape, although I am not much heavier than in my playing days. That's down to the worry more than anything else.'

Despite his unmitigated success, O'Neill was adamant his squad were ahead of themselves in terms of achievement and had not yet fulfilled their potential. He continued: 'The title will go all the way to a Sunday finish as Rangers will make themselves stronger than last season. The game is fickle and changes from week to week, never mind from season to season. That is what's responsible for the removal of so many managers. And I should know – I was responsible for the removal of a few of them myself when I was a player. Yesterday's hero can quickly turn into yesterday's forgotten man. I know there is an intensity of feeling that attaches itself to Celtic, but I also understand that I will be judged even more harshly. When I became Celtic manager the club had lost the league to Rangers by twenty-one points. If I had cut the gap to eight or nine points and finished as runner-up in my first season in charge I would have still regarded that as being progress of a kind. The fans would have been content, but they would be looking for more significant progress next season, so what is the difference. I consider myself to be a dreamer by nature but a confirmed realist when it comes to my professional duties. My job is to win games and realise that I can't keep all the players happy doing what I think is best to get those victories.'

Being manager of an Old Firm side meant either elation or disappointment so O'Neill could not afford to rest on his laurels as Rangers overhauled their squad in the close season. While O'Neill's turnaround at Parkhead had been miraculous, it would have been naïve to think Rangers were not capable of an equally rapid comeback. That was the constant pressure O'Neill experienced while he was at the helm of Celtic Football Club.

'Second season syndrome' has plagued both managers and clubs alike. Once managers and clubs had a year to assess the style and temperament of O'Neill's side, the question was: could they sustain it? Rangers had replaced Dick Advocaat with the impressive young Scottish manager Alex McLeish, hoping to inject some energy into the Ibrox club. Despite being Scottish champions Celtic were forced to contend with Ajax for a place in the group stages of the Champions League. It was certainly not the easiest draw for O'Neill's men. An incredible 3-1 win in the Dutch capital sent Celtic well on their way to qualification and, despite a 1-0 loss at Parkhead, Martin O'Neill and his side would have their first crack at Europe's premier club competition. O'Neill believed his side were good value for a place in the group stages, with the Celtic coffers considerably swelled by the £10 million bonus. The six group matches would be six cup finals, according to the Ulsterman, and he was adamant his side would have a good go at any of the European elite.

Celtic were drawn alongside Porto, Rosenborg and Italian giants Juventus in the group stages and gave a good account of themselves, beating both Porto and Rosenborg while suffering a heartbreaking 3-2 defeat at the Stadio della Alpi, Juventus' imposing Turin home. Disappointing performances on the road, however, hampered Celtic's campaign, meaning qualification from the group would go right to the wire. O'Neill was aware that, having won the SPL title with ease the season before, juggling a successful

Champions League campaign with their domestic commitments would be his biggest challenge. Indeed such was the confidence in the Celtic side that they battled back from two goals behind against Juventus, and were beaten only be a dubious penalty. O'Neill was suitably displeased and hit with a one-game touchline ban for his protests.

As the season moved into October, Celtic would have the chance for revenge as they welcomed the Italians to Parkhead, knowing qualification for the second phase of the competition was still a possibility. Allessandro del Piero and David Trezeguet all found the back of the net for Juve, but Joos Valgaeren, Henrik Larsson and a Chris Sutton brace gave Celtic a famous 4-3 win on an amazing night at Parkhead. O'Neill was aware his European heroes had the character to go far in European competition, and were not intimidated by the biggest club's on the continent. While Celtic had done their part in beating Juve, Rosenborg failed to take points off Porto, and the Portuguese side took their place in the second round of the competition. It was a bitter blow. 'The UEFA Cup is a great competition, it will be a great experience,' a disappointed O'Neill commented. 'We tried for the fans, but it was disappointing at the end of the evening, that is the way it goes.'

Certainly Celtic found little difficulty on the domestic stage and began the 2001/2002 season with the same ruthless streak as the year before. A surprise goalless draw with Livingston in August was the only blip in a blistering start in the SPL. Celtic would need to win the division in order to qualify for next year's Champions League, making the league an absolute priority for O'Neill and the Bhoys. But there was still the UEFA Cup, and a third-round tie with Valencia, to contest. The Spanish side had plenty of flair players and were holding their own in the fiercely competitive Spanish league. With Pablo Aimar, Roberto Ayala and the giant John Carew, they would pose a stern test of Celtic's European credentials. The first leg, at the Mestalla, went the way of the home side as Vicente's late goal settled a typically close game, fiercely contested by Celtic. The return leg a fortnight later would prove crucial for O'Neill and Celtic Park was rocking. Henrik Larsson netted the game's only goal, sending the tie into extra time. Despite an extra half an hour of play, the teams could not be separated, sending the game into a penalty shoot out. Unfortunately for O'Neill, it was the Spaniards who triumphed, leaving the Ulsterman wondering what might have been. 'I thought it was an immense performance by the players and we deserved to go through not just after 90 minutes but also 120 minutes,' he said. 'When it comes to penalties it is obviously a lottery but its part of the rules. We have played against a side that got to the finals of the Champions League in the last two years and I thought we were much, much better than them on the night.'

So domestic success would have to satisfy O'Neill and in fact it was not until December that Celtic tasted defeat as Aberdeen took the points at Pittodrie. 'What it does illustrate is that the league is far from over,' O'Neill said after the defeat. 'We have only reached the half way stage. It was inevitable because you cannot just keep winning.' But Celtic were the runaway leaders, with victories over

Rangers confirming their dominance in the division. They were also easing through the knockout competitions, hitting eight past Stirling Albion in the League Cup and five past Alloa to ensure cup football into 2002. By early February Celtic had battled through to the semi-final of the league cup, the first of three trophies Martin O'Neill was defending this season. In a repeat of last year's semi-final, Celtic met Rangers for a place in the competition's showpiece but this time it was Rangers who progressed after extra time. It was a bitter blow for O'Neill, who was rightly proud of Celtic's league cup success and gutted to surrender a trophy. It was rare for O'Neill to have to pick his players up after defeat, but there was still plenty to play for. He felt Celtic had dominated the game but crucial missed chances cost the Bhoys dearly.

If they needed any extra motivation, defeat was something they would not taste in the league for the remainder of the season in the SPL. Celtic's defence was proving just as effective as their attack, and many sides in the SPL were struggling to break down the Bhoys' rearguard. While Rangers held Celtic to a 1-1 draw in an Old Firm clash in March, Dunfermline, Dundee and Aberdeen were all swept aside as Martin O'Neill's men continued their relentless march towards the title. Indeed the league was all but over as a contest by March, with Rangers' failure to take maximum points both a psychological and physical blow. Alex McLeish's side could not get near them. Celtic wrapped up the title with ease, reaching the 100 point mark before the final game of the season. But there was still the small matter of a

Scottish FA Cup final against the old enemy. Cup success would not ease the pain of another embarrassing campaign in the SPL, but the chance to take one trophy away from Parkhead would be some small consolation for Rangers. A last-minute goal from Peter Lovenkrands won the game for Rangers, when the game seemed destined for extra time with the teams deadlocked at two apiece. The jubilant Rangers players knew they had landed a body blow. But O'Neill had his place in the Champions League, and refused to get too downhearted. While he admitted tiredness was a factor, O'Neill was not too hard on his players. 'I would have to say the loss doesn't bother me other than the fact we lost the game. Next season is next season.'

The 2001/02 season, while not as trophy laden as the year before, had taught O'Neill and his squad plenty of lessons. With a taste for Champions League football, it was clear that European football would be the final frontier for Celtic. And O'Neill was desperate for success.

CHAPTER 7

THE ROAD TO SEVILLE

'It was very tense for me. In fact, I can't remember being quite so nervous since my old days going to the discotheque when I had to explain why I was getting home at three in the morning – that was just as stressful.'

If his treble-winning 2000/01 season had been a miracle and the 2001/02 season had been a year of consolidation, then the 2002/03 season turned out to be a rollercoaster ride the Celtic supporters would never forget.

Having competed against European giants Juventus in the previous season's Champions League, O'Neill was desperate to savour more great nights at Parkhead against the continent's elite. Standing in the way were Swiss side Basel in a qualifying tie, and the double-header added extra spice to the August programme in the summer of 2002. Basel travelled to Celtic Park for the first leg with a side, bereft of any real star names, that was unlikely to make an impression in the group stages later on in the season. The visitors, however, got off to a dream start, netting inside two minutes, but

Celtic stormed back, netting three without reply to leave the tie delicately balanced: Basel's away goal ensured the Bhoys would have an uncomfortable trip to Switzerland. Celtic had been indebted to under-fire goalkeeper Rab Douglas, who had pulled off a couple of inspired saves to keep the visitors at bay, and, after the game, O'Neill made a point of not counting out the Swiss side, commenting: 'We did well to come back, but they got the away goal they had come for and Basel are, without doubt, a decent side. Anybody calling this tie over and done with is out by a long way. These ties come so early in the season, but they are so, so important. It is what you do on the evening that counts.'

Tragically for Celtic, however, it was Basel who took the initiative in the second leg, securing a 2-0 win that saw them progress on the away-goals rule. The defeat cost Celtic Football Club somewhere in the region of £10 million and ensured another season competing in the UEFA Cup – very much a consolation prize for the league champions. But while ties against Valencia, Juventus and Rosenborg may no longer have been a possibility, the reality was that, for a team low in European confidence, the UEFA Cup represented a better chance of silverware.

O'Neill was more than aware that the early exit from the Champions League would mean an inevitable lack of transfer funds. In the post-mortem examination, he said: 'We didn't get the result and that will play a part in proceedings over the next few days – it is very disappointing in terms of the financial clout of the club. We spend ten hard months winning the league to take our place in the qualifying round, but we will now try and come again next season for the Champions League. I am disappointed. We are in the UEFA Cup, but it could have been so much better for us. In the second half we had some great chances and their keeper made three point-blank saves. But it wasn't our night. We didn't make the best of starts and we conceded two bad goals from our point of view. That they came from set-pieces is particularly disappointing, but we will pick ourselves up.'

Aware that the defeat would have major implications on Celtic's season, O'Neill dodged questions regarding his own future after the Champions League failure. There was major criticism in the press following the defeat, with Basel labelled a 'pub team', something O'Neill was quick to refute. 'If Basel are the pub team I heard them being described as when they played us, then they are the best pub team I have ever seen,' he said. 'They have also shown they are a better side than they have been given credit for being by some people. A combination of bad luck and good goalkeeping stopped us from getting the result we needed on their ground.'

A dominant start to the SPL campaign (they won their opening five matches) helped ease the pain of the Champions League disappointment, but Celtic trailed Rangers by four points by the time their UEFA Cup campaign got underway in September. O'Neill's side were drawn against Lithuanian side FK Suduva and would play the first leg at Parkhead. O'Neill told the *Sunday Express*: 'We have had Suduva watched and we are capable of winning this tie – but we have no divine right to win.'

Ulrik Larsson, a typically classy O'Neill summer signing from Hibernian, admitted the pressure felt by the Celtic players. 'Everyone expects Celtic to win most of their games and that is the pressure you feel because you know there are good players out there besides the Old Firm who, on their day, can be a threat to us. But this is a huge club and you have to keep getting results to stay huge...When I first came to Scotland the talk was all about Rangers' dominance; and then Celtic won the treble followed by the championship again and that raises expectations. But it is better that people expect you to win the title than be relegated.'

O'Neill admitted an air of disappointment had hung around Parkhead for too long and that the atmosphere had become flat. But a new European challenge lay ahead for Celtic and he intended to grab it with both hands. 'The supporters are edgy,' he told *The Sun*. 'We can't afford to dwell on it any more – we have to move on. I have been the worst with it – I do take time, but it is time to get on with life. In our last European home tie against Basel we simply got off to a bad start and we have to try and avoid that this time. I look at Manchester United and Arsenal and they are miles ahead of us in terms of what they have done. Untied had five goes at the Champions League before they won it and Arsenal are into their fifth attempt – yet they have never gone beyond the last eight. The football is very hard and I don't need the results to tell me how difficult it will be.'

O'Neill accepted that European heavyweights such as United or Real Madrid could take their place in the Champions League proper for granted, but that Celtic were still in their infancy on the European stage and would need more experience. He continued in the *Mirror*: 'We certainly don't have that arrogance and we know games are difficult. You have got to be physically right and mentally right. I saw the tapes of the Suduva games against Brann and they can play a bit. They can look after themselves, but they like to play. I have seen they have mixed it up a bit, they went long and they went short.'

O'Neill need not have worried, as, much to the delight of the fans who had had little to cheer on the European stage since victory over Basel in August, Celtic smashed eight past their hapless opponents. Champions League pain was now well and truly behind them. A dominant performance, led, predictably, by Henrik Larsson (who scored a hat-trick), proved the perfect tonic for the jaded Celtic supporters. O'Neill told the *Mirror*: 'I will now consider giving some of the younger lads European experience. It would be pretty feasible now. I have got a number of players I would like to see in action and this gives them that opportunity.' The return tie represented an equally easy ride for the Bhoys and, following a comfortable 2-0 victory, they secured a place in the next round.

Little had changed in the SPL, with Rangers still leading the way, but Celtic had won their game in hand on the league leaders and now trailed by just a single point with twelve games played. Successive 4-1 wins over Hearts and Dunfermline, lead inevitably by Henrik Larsson, kept Celtic in touch with a much-improved Rangers, who were desperate to avoid the embarrassment of defeat for a third year running.

The next stop on Celtic's grand journey through the competition would see Scottish manager Graham Souness bring his Blackburn Rovers side north of the border for a potentially volatile home nations derby at the end of October. Ahead of the game, Souness admitted he was expecting a rough reception in Glasgow, telling the *Mirror*: 'I know I will need my old tin hat when I go back to Celtic – it won't be the first time I have needed it in my career and it probably won't be the last. I am looking forward to going back and meeting my fellow Scotsmen again – whatever they throw at me.'

The Battle of Britain reignited the brief flirtation with moving the Old Firm to the Premier League, but O'Neill was adamant the knockout competition would have no bearing on the debate. 'If we win it won't really prove anything regarding whether or not Scottish teams like Celtic and Rangers are good enough to play in the Premiership. It won't prove anything except this is a big competition and one we would obviously like to get through, but I am sure Blackburn are feeling exactly the same way. They have got good players; they have spent a few bob down through the years and have done recently. They have a good side without a doubt. They won the League Cup last season; they can play a bit and have some very talented players. I suppose people will ask how we measure up against Premiership opposition and all that kind of thing, and it will be a difficult game for us. When I knew the six sides that we could be paired with I knew that it was an absolute certainty we would get Blackburn. It is a very difficult tie for us, without a doubt, but it is one we can look forward to. The travelling support is immense and there will be a full house at Celtic Park, so it is one to savour.'

For O'Neill and Souness, the tie gave them the opportunity to pit their managerial wits against each other, just as they had done as players several decades past. O'Neill's Nottingham Forest and Souness's Liverpool served up some legendary matches in the late 1970s. O'Neill fondly recalled: 'They ended our forty-two-match unbeaten run,' he fondly recalled to the *Daily Mail*. 'As a player Graeme was, how can I put this, aggressive. But he was a very good player and very influential in that Liverpool team. We had Ian Bowyer, who could not only look after himself and other cloggers in the team, but he could also look after the Liverpool players. But they had Graeme and the matches between the two sides were just terrific. We had the Indian Sign over Liverpool for a couple of years.'

But it was at Rangers where Souness would have his biggest effect on the Scottish game. O'Neill continued: 'He was terrific for football in Scotland. That was the first time you had ever seen a migration of English players into the Scottish League. I had forgotten, actually, that the ban on English clubs competing in Europe was a factor at the time, but he certainly shifted the emphasis and made Rangers a real power again. He also blew away the pay ceiling.'

At Blackburn, Souness had reunited Dwight Yorke and Andy Cole, a deadly strike partnership that had fired Manchester United to Champions League glory in 1999.

Though a few years had passed since that glorious night in Barcelona, O'Neill admitted the pair's pedigree would be enough to warrant concern from any side. He told the *Daily Record*: 'We are talking about coming up against a partnership with European Cup-winners' medals to their names. They have scored goals in any company in the past and I am sure they will do so again in the future. When I looked at the teams we could have faced in this round of the UEFA Cup then there is no doubt they are the best partnership that could have come up against us. But it is a challenge for us to stop them and progress to the next round. Souness has brought them to the club to help them into Europe, rather than fight relegation. He will also be looking to them to help win this game against us, there is no doubt we will have to be on top of our game to stop them in both games.'

Stoking the fire ahead of the game, O'Neill added: 'No matter what I think, the comparisons will be drawn [between the English and Scottish leagues] and eventually we will be made out to represent Scotland. I hope for Scottish football secondly, but for Celtic Football Club, firstly that we come through this tie. People will inevitably draw comparisons because they are going well in the Premiership and they are up against a team who have been talked about moving down and people will be interested to see how we cope. I am not too sure that two games will tell you exactly where we would stand if we were to go down there. That is the big argument. They are playing competitive football every single week in the Premiership.'

The Souness versus O'Neill rivalry, intensified by the Battle of Britain talk in the media, dredged up a memory that still caused unease to the Ulsterman. During his playing days, a horror tackle by Souness had started a downward spiral that had brought about a premature end to O'Neill's career.

A solitary goal from Henrik Larsson was enough to give Celtic a slender advantage after the first leg at Celtic Park, but O'Neill was angered by critics who claimed Celtic had used a 'long-ball tactic' to win the game, telling the *Express*: 'Is there a situation where we can ever win here? We have won a game. I always thought that professional football was about winningm for a start. The funny thing is, if we go down and get through, there will be one or two moans from down south saying: "It just shows you, Blackburn couldn't go through." But if we go through, I don't care. People will say whatever they want, but we have won a game, which I think is sometimes forgotten. We have had to adjust to a tempo we aren't used to. We were absolutely splendid in our comeback against Basel at Parkhead; we had a fantastic game against Juventus last season and a fantastic game against Valencia where we played them off the pitch. I don't remember comments on the way we went out. Don't get me wrong, the performance is always important, but all of my players have got to take fantastic credit from the game.'

Blackburn boss Graham Souness earned the wrath of O'Neill by claiming Blackburn were technically superior to Celtic and how his side had not got what they deserved in the first leg. This certainly irked O'Neill who was forced to hear pundits share similar sentiments about his side and the manner of their win over Blackburn. 'I'm too old now to concern myself with what other people are always thinking. Am I really trying to please some discerning viewer in London? Sorry, I'm out to try and win the game. Ideally I would want to win it with a bit of panache but sometimes the two might not go together.'

Despite holding a slender lead, Celtic still needed to make the trip to Ewood Park, and O'Neill knew his side would need to draw on their best European performances to get a result. 'It is the kind of form that we showed against Ajax in the Champions League qualifiers last season – or the kind of displays we gave home and away against Juventus,' he said. 'If we play anything like the way we did while going out to Valencia in the UEFA Cup [last season], I am confident we will go through against Blackburn. I had no pretensions that we could win the Champions League last season and I have no pretensions where the UEFA Cup is concerned this time. But I will be disappointed if we don't go through to the next round. It won't wreck our season if Celtic don't make it, but the club will start to make money out of the tournament if we can reach the quarter-final stage.'

The second leg, a fortnight later, proved a much more comfortable outing for O'Neill's men, who enjoyed a welcome win on their travels in Europe. Goals either side of half-time from Henrik Larsson and Chris Sutton secured a memorable result for Celtic, who progressed with a comfortable 3-0 scoreline over the two legs. Following the win, O'Neill sent out a statement of intent to Celtic's UEFA

Always part of the team: Martin displays some of his ball-handling prowess at the Celtic training ground.

Family comes first for Martin. He received an OBE on 16 July, 2004 and is pictured here with his wife, Geraldine and daughters Aisling (*left*), 22, and Alana, 20.

Above and below left: Celtic fans show their support at the Tennent's Scottish FA Cup Final against Dundee United in 2005.

Below right: Martin celebrates a Celtic goal.

Above: A well-loved manager. Martin meets and greets some of his Celtic fans.

Below: Draped in the Celtic colours, Martin gives the fans a big thumbs up.

Above: Celtic celebrate winning after beating Dundee United in the Scottish FA Cup final on 28 May, 2005.

Below: Winning the trophy provided an emotional sending off for the departing manager. Martin O'Neill left to care for his wife Geraldine, who had lymphoma.

Martin poses with Aston Villa chairman Doug Ellis as he is named their new manager. His appointment at Aston Villa signalled the end of Martin's 15-month hiatus from the sport.

Above: Martin restrains his player Gabriel Agbonlahor as his team clashes with the Bolton Wanderers on 3 April, 2010.

Below: Two managers square off: Aston Villa's Martin O'Neill with Liverpool's Rafael Benitez.

Aston Villa's time under Martin O'Neill has been full of glorious highs and frustrating lows but one thing is for certain – Martin O'Neill remains one of the most respected managers in football today.

Cup rivals. He told gathered reporters: 'I am pleased to be in the hat. I am pleased to be in it and if Leeds or Liverpool come out then it would not bother me. It doesn't mean we will win it, but they will be games to look forward to, I am quite sure. The players were up for the game and they took some criticism. We took a lot of criticism for the first game and I had to remind myself that we actually won the game when I went home. I am delighted we won. It doesn't make us the best team in the world, but it doesn't make us the side people suggested we were.'

On the domestic front, Celtic had been on terrific form but their defence had been unusually porous, losing 2-1 to Motherwell in September before an entertaining 3-3 draw with Rangers. Still, O'Neill's side remained firmly in touch with their title rivals. Perhaps European pressures were beginning to affect the Celtic squad, which O'Neill accepted was not the biggest.

The SPL was proving to be one of the most frantic campaigns in recent years and Celtic were able to snatch first place by the end of November with a series of comfortable wins, including a spectacular 7-0 thrashing of Aberdeen. O'Neill had feared the small Celtic squad would struggle to cope with the rigours of European football and they were forced to show their battling qualities when slogging it out with Rangers for top spot. It was turning into a fascinating battle.

O'Neill's bold claim that he did not care who came out of the hat was put to the test when Celta Vigo were drawn in the third round of the competition. O'Neill told *The Times*: 'We didn't get much time to enjoy that win over

Blackburn. In fact, it was similar to last year, when we beat Juventus here 4-3 in the Champions League and then found out Rosenborg had missed a sitter in the last minute at Porto that would have kept us in the competition. Even though we had gone down into the UEFA Cup, this place was still pretty euphoric. Then, we finished training on Friday and learned we had drawn Valencia. The draw could have been kinder to us. Of the four teams we were bracketed with in the draw, Celta Vigo were the hardest. I would expect them to be a very strong side, and if they are perhaps not on a par with Valencia, if you are in the top four of the Spanish League you are a good side.' But the victory over Blackburn had been a satisfying one, especially given some of the comments from south of the border regarding the style of Celtic's victory, particularly in the first leg.

Celta Vigo, who had enjoyed a stunning season in Spain in 2001/02, boasted Edu, Alexandre Mostovoi and Gustavo Lopez in their side. The technically gifted players represented a much different challenge to the physical and tenacious Blackburn side. Beating Celta Vigo would keep Celtic in European competition beyond Christmas, something they had not achieved in twenty-three years, but, ahead of the game, O'Neill urged caution, telling *The Times*: 'British teams do not have a great record against Spanish sides. Even Manchester United, who are Champions League perennials, do not have a clever record. The night we had against Valencia here last season was fantastic. We could have won it in extra-time. It was draining to watch the penalty shoot-out, but it remains a great experience. The UEFA Cup is not like the Champions League, where if you concede a goal in a group match, it is not the end of the world. It is like being back to the old European format, where the away goal is very important.'

The first leg, at Parkhead, was a fiery affair, but nowhere more so than in the Celtic dugout, where O'Neill was controversially sent off by French referee Claude Columbo. The incident, in the closing minutes of the match, could not overshadow a brilliant 1-0 win for the Bhoys on home turf. 'It was inappropriate, without a doubt,' O'Neill told the *Scotsman*. 'There is probably no chance of doing anything about it, but I would certainly want to send some video evidence, not only of that particular incident, but of the game itself. Maybe the referee, at his leisure, could have a look at it before he starts putting his own official report on the game. There is a basic difference from the Juventus game last year in that I wasn't out of my technical area this time. The referee came over to ask the fourth official: "Was he complaining about me?" The linesman just shrugged his shoulders and actually said: "No". The referee decided to go ahead with it anyway.'

It seemed bitterness would follow Celtic home and away on their magical European tour, as Vigo coach Miguel Angel Lotina delivered a damning verdict on the side. He said: 'I was quite happy with the referee as he was quite balanced for both teams. I was not very impressed by Celtic and they did not surprise me at all. The crowd impressed me very much, but the 60,000 Celtic fans will not be in Vigo for the second match. I expected a better result, but I am happy with what my team have done.'

O'Neill, meanwhile, responded: 'I couldn't care less what some coach says about us and he should worry about his own team. That is his job. It was obvious we deserved to win tonight and obvious that we played better than Celta Vigo – who are a good side. I was delighted with the performance and if there was a disappointment, it was that we didn't get the second goal that would have been just reward for the way we played. We were terrific and the performance is up there with beating Valencia last year.'

O'Neill was certainly frustrated. After beating Blackburn his side had come in for criticism for their handling of the tie and he was stoic in the face of fresh criticism from his opposite number.

Celtic, lead by an enigmatic boss, were a hard-working side who gave 100 per cent in both domestic and European competition. But they had come under fire for their approach to the game, with pundits and opposition managers alike keen to have their say on Martin O'Neill's Celtic. The Ulsterman found it a constant source of frustration. There was plenty of bad feeling following Celtic around Europe, but O'Neill would always leap to the defence of his players. Winning was all that mattered.

While O'Neill's dismissal in a typically vociferous outburst would see him watch the crucial second leg from the stands, he maintained he was not aware of what he had done to merit the sending off and protested his innocence from the start. He had the opportunity to fight his corner with UEFA and insisted he would have gone to a hearing regardless of the date or time. Fortunately, Europe's governing body sided with the Ulsterman, though it went without saying that he would need to be on best behaviour in the Balaidos Stadium for the December rematch.

Celtic were greeted by a wall of noise as they set out to protect their slender one-goal advantage at the stadium. And the game got off to a disastrous start for O'Neill's men as they fell behind to a 24th-minute strike. However, John Hartson responded in the 37th minute to give Celtic a crucial away goal – meaning Vigo would need to score twice. In a nerve-shredding second half, the home side only managed to score one, through South African forward Benni McCarthy, putting Celtic through to the last sixteen on away goals. Barely able to contain his delight, O'Neill told the *Express*: 'We have created history tonight by getting through to the last sixteen and we will need to put that aside for now. We will enjoy tonight for a couple of hours. I thought we were fantastic – it was a great effort.'

Back on the domestic front, December had been a month of frustration for O'Neill. Draws with Kilmarnock and Aberdeen handed the initiative back to Rangers, who stood on top by a solitary point as the season moved into the New Year. With no European football until the end of February, it was to be a crucial spell. A draw against Aberdeen in the first match of 2003 was the only blip for Celtic, who produced a series of efficient, if unspectacular performances. However, going into the next round of European games, on February 20, Rangers had opened up a six point lead, though Celtic had a crucial game in hand that kept the title within their grasp – and heaped added importance on the Old Firm games, which would decide the fate of the league title.

German side Stuttgart would be Celtic's last-sixteen opponents, with the winners going on to face either Liverpool or Auxerre in the quarter-finals. However, despite having their odds slashed to win the title, O'Neill insisted his side would go into the tie against the Bundesliga outfit as underdogs. He told the *Mirror*: 'Stuttgart are doing well in the Bundesliga, another strong and competitive league, and I think we can expect another severe test – although whoever you get at this stage of the tournament will be tough opponents. As for Liverpool, don't even talk about it! The most important thing for us is to concentrate on this game and this one only... Stuttgart will go into the game as favourites, but we have a bit of confidence and will be positive. It was a fantastic achievement for us to beat a Spanish side, something we have never done. Last year we were put out on penalties by the eventual Spanish champions and it was nice to go through against a team who are riding high in La Liga. To be able to look forward to European football after Christmas is fantastic and something we will enjoy.'

By early 2003, Celtic's UEFA Cup run was in full flow and the club was enjoying European football beyond Christmas for the first time in a quarter of a century. However, with just six months left to run on his contract at Parkhead, questions began to arise over O'Neill's future. O'Neill believed Celtic's hesitation in offering him a new contract was a sign that his services were no longer required and felt as though he was within his rights to go searching for his next step on the managerial ladder. He signed an agreement in principle with Peter Ridsdale, by no means a binding legal contract, but enough to make the former Leeds supremo confident he would finally snare his man. The situation at Elland Road was certainly not as rosy as it had been when O'Neill was at Leicester. Mounting debts had forced the Yorkshire club to sell off many of its prized assets, including Robbie Keane and Rio Ferdinand, and boss Terry Venables would soon threaten to walk if defender Jonathan Woodgate was offloaded as well. Speculation in the press that O'Neill had held secret talks with Ridsdale the previous summer when David O'Leary finally departed, was rife, something the Ulsterman strenuously denied. Considering his open and honest approach to the Leeds job, O'Neill's outrage at this latest round of speculation spoke volumes. He told the *Daily Record*: 'When I signed my three-year agreement I said that unless the Celtic board saw fit to part company with me I would see that contract through to the end. I have honoured every single one of the terms and conditions laid down in that contract. The board have known everything that was going on. If you are asking me was I going to leave before my term in office was over, then my answer is that I was always staying at Celtic Park.'

Leaving in the summer of 2002 would have broken the terms of his Celtic contract, and perhaps, more importantly, O'Neill's self-imposed rule of never breaking a contract where possible. However, by the New Year, just months remained on his Celtic deal and he could not be confident improved terms would be forthcoming. Cue Peter Ridsdale with another proposition.

'I would like to put it in context,' O'Neill told the *Birmingham Evening Post*. 'Peter was the chairman at Leeds who tried to sign me in 1998 and Leicester City would not give me permission to speak formally about the position at Leeds. David O'Leary took over and did very well indeed, and then when David was leaving Peter asked me again in 2002, by which time I was manager of Celtic. Two years had gone into a three-year deal. Obviously he spoke to the Celtic board and, after a bit of deliberation, the Celtic board said they would not give them permission to speak to me. That was absolutely fine, because I was enjoying it at Celtic immensely. Two years had gone on the contract and I had another to run at that stage. Then, when it was running down with some months left, Peter approached me again and, at this stage, Terry Venables was in charge, but Peter told me Terry was wishing to leave and he would want to go at the end of the season. At this stage Celtic had not offered me a contract and I was within my rights to go and look for employment after the end of June 2003. Peter pleaded with me. Thinking Celtic no longer wanted my services at the end of my contract, obviously I was free to speak to anyone. I said in principle I would go there, obviously under quite a number of conditions – though not financial conditions at all, by any stretch of the imagination.

'Peter Ridsdale wanted me as manager and did approach me a couple of times – first in 1998, when I wasn't allowed to speak to them which was fine, then again in 2002,' he continued. 'I had originally signed a three-year contract in 2000. I was into the last few months of my contract and there hadn't been any discussions about a new deal. There had been no talk about it at all, so I just assumed they wanted me to see my three years out at that time.'

O'Neill felt he was within his rights to speak to Leeds as he was in the last few months of a deal with no new offer. He spoke to Peter who asked to see him.

'He has mentioned that we met to go through loads of contractual details, but that was not the case. I think some statement of intent was drawn up subject to quite a few conditions – one of which was that Peter told me that then-Leeds manager Terry Venables wanted to leave. It was not a contract as such and certainly not a legal document, but Peter was saying he needed something to show his board there was serious intent from me. I was happy to do that because I had to see if I had the potential to be working after 30 June 2003, when my Celtic contract was due to expire. When I realised what Peter had said to me at the meeting had not stacked up, I spoke to Celtic owner Dermot Desmond and it became clear Celtic did actually want me to stay on. It turned out the board had felt there was a bit of an understanding and that my relationship with Dermot was such that he would get around to drawing up a new contract at some stage. As the conditions Peter Ridsdale promised were not adhered to, I wrote to him to tell him I would not now take the position.'

Ridsdale, meanwhile, maintained he was as sure as he could be that O'Neill would finally take up the Elland

Road hot seat. The later release of his book, *United We Fall*, in 2007, dredged up old memories and some of the revelations in it had to be strenuously denied by O'Neill. 'This really is old hat, but I suppose Peter has a book to write,' O'Neill said. 'I believed, when I spoke to Dermot, that the misunderstanding was cleared up. I went on to sign a one-year rolling contract [with Celtic].'

Forced to defend the accusations in his book, Ridsdale said: 'I was sure of the man I wanted at Leeds. I approached Martin O'Neill three times about the job. He is an outstanding manager. The truth hurts. There are some people, who when they see the truth, either deny it or try to reinvent it. I cannot be 100 per cent convinced Martin O'Neill would have joined Leeds because it had not been announced, even though he had given us the authorisation to do so, but I stand by my belief he would. But Martin always said we were destined to work together. We had already tried twice, so why would he come down to see me. Why would he and Geraldine sit and have dinner with myself and my wife? Why would he sign the contract? Martin is one of the most loyal managers I know. To suggest I somehow coerced him into signing a contract just does him a disservice. He is a far stronger man than that.'

'It shows how little strength was in the letter from Peter Ridsdale.' O'Neill added: 'It was full of conditions that I later found to be untrue – I even spoke to Terry Venables later and he said he had no intention of giving up his job. I did not want to leave Celtic. I loved the football club. If truth be told, I was disappointed about their failure to offer me a new deal. It was the first time Celtic had played

European football and still been in the tournament after Christmas for twenty-six years. We were also still heavily involved with and challenging for our third Scottish Premier League championship. I was a bit disappointed with the delay, but then the misunderstanding was cleared up and I was happy to go with it. There is no doubt I would have had a serious interest in the Leeds job, but I want fans to understand that I did not want to leave Celtic and, had the new deal been forthcoming earlier, I would never have looked elsewhere. I would like to think my record at all the football clubs I have been at speaks for itself when it comes to honouring contracts. I only ever once broke a contract and that was at Norwich City to join Leicester City and that is something I regret. Had things been different on the home front, I might never have left Celtic at all.'

Stuttgart travelled to Parkhead on 20 February to face Celtic for the first leg of the last-sixteen clash boosted by the news that prolific hitman Henrik Larsson would miss the match. O'Neill's preparations were further dented when the previous league match against Motherwell was postponed. O'Neill confessed it was a real blow to the side, but insisted Celtic's fellow strikers would have to step up to the plate and prove they could cover for the Swede. According to the Ulsterman, Stuttgart's preparations had not been ideal either; he claimed they had not officially sent a scout to watch them. O'Neill commented in the *Evening Times*: 'So far Stuttgart have not sent anyone – certainly not through Celtic – to watch us. Normally, the done thing is for a club to contact us so that we can arrange for their representatives to be looked after in terms of tickets, accommodation and the like. To my knowledge, Stuttgart haven't done so. That doesn't mean they have not sent a scout or contact to watch us, but it would be a strange way to do things. It would amaze me, though, if they went into the game having only watched us on video. If so, I would suspect they don't really know our capabilities.'

The nightmare lead-up to the match continued when goalkeeper Magnus Hedman suffered an injury just days before the game. But injuries were not Celtic's only problem: O'Neill, still serving a dug-out ban, would be unable to interact with his players throughout the duration of the match. Confident in the ability of his coaching team, he told the *Mirror*: 'I prefer to be in the technical area, but I will be in the stand trying to behave myself. When I was banned from the touchline for the Porto game last season people were saying that I would get a better view – but I prefer to be 20 yards nearer the pitch. The team talk will be a bit earlier than normal, but the players will be up for the game.'

Once again, Celtic were forced to come from a goal behind after German international Kevin Kuranyi's 27th-minute strike sent Stuttgart – already down to ten men after the 17th-minute dismissal of Marcelo Bordon for a professional foul – into an unexpected lead. But the Hoops wasted little time in getting an equaliser, courtesy of Paul Lambert. Shaun Maloney and Stilian Petrov added goals each side of half-time to cap a wonderful European performance for O'Neill's side – who sat delighted in the stands. The Ulsterman was aware his side had thrown away a two-goal advantage this season in a performance against Basel that had banished them to the UEFA Cup and O'Neill was adamant it would not happen again. He told the *Scotsman*: 'It does not unfortunately follow because it has happened once that it won't happen again. I would have settled for this beforehand, especially after they scored. We had major players out of the team so we can take confidence from this game, but it is over now. There is no great euphoria in the dressing room. They are pleased within themselves. Stuttgart have been flying recently and made some adjustments after the player was sent off and within ten minutes found themselves in front. I think we switched off, perhaps thinking the extra man might count.'

Speaking of his touchline ban, he added: 'It is not a place I want to spend the rest of my life. It is frustrating, but perhaps I am learning my lesson, although I am not saying I won't be back there. A German TV crew said there is a lot of talk about an all-British quarter-final. Not from me. Not from any of the players.'

The mouth-watering prospect of a quarter-final against Liverpool would have been enough motivation for the Celtic players, but their boss was insistent they could still end up out of the competition following the game in Germany. He told *The Times*: 'We have done well in the UEFA Cup because of the disappointment of Basel. The experience in Switzerland, where they went out on the away-goals rule after surrendering a 3-1 first-leg lead, will be in tempering wild optimism in Germany. The one thing

Basel did was to ensure that no Celtic fan could possibly be thinking about Liverpool in the quarter-finals. I have seen the occasional smile on the faces of the directors when they think of the money to be made. The quarter-final could be worth £1 million – but that is not my concern. I saw enough at Celtic Park, especially in the early stages, to know they can cause us problems. This is a club that was in the Cup-Winners' Cup final in 1998 and now they have a young side which is third in the Bundesliga.'

Celtic travelled to the Gottlieb-Daimler stadium, Stuttgart's impressive home, on 27 February knowing an away goal would swing the tie even further in their favour. In fact, they got two, with Alan Thompson and Chris Sutton both netting inside the opening 15 minutes to give Celtic a dream start. Three goals from the Germans were not enough to prevent the Bhoys from progressing to a dream quarter-final with Liverpool. O'Neill spoke of his immense pride: 'We felt we had to score. To score two goals and for them to go through was a big ask. But to me the disconcerting thing was the goal we conceded before half-time. If we could have gone through [to half-time without conceding that goal] we could have perhaps won the game. It was a lapse of concentration on our part, but to go through is the most important thing. If you had told me the scoreline before I would have taken it. I am obviously delighted to be in the quarter-final of the UEFA Cup. Over the two games we deserved to win, but I have to say that Stuttgart showed why they are lying third in the Bundesliga.'

Speaking of their opponents lying just south of the

border, he added: 'Closer to the time I will give it plenty of thought. I suppose there will be all sorts of comparisons made. They are a talented side and we will give it our best shot. Michael Owen is a top-class player and it will be nice to see Emile Heskey, who did wonderfully well for me at Leicester, again. I will concern myself with that closer to the time. It is a great tie for us and we will try and defend a wee bit better than we did in the last ten minutes or so here. Liverpool are a top-class side and I am surprised with the way they fell away in the league, especially after being in a wonderful position early on. They are definitely coming back to form and have quality players all over the field. We will be underdogs, but we will give it everything.'

If the Liverpool tie was proving a distraction for O'Neill's men, they didn't show it as they beat Rangers 1-0 the weekend before their mammoth European tie. Despite taking three points off their title rivals, Rangers still held a three point lead, but O'Neill knew Celtic still had a game in hand, meaning goal difference could play a massive part in the domestic campaign.

The first leg of the eagerly anticipated European clash, dubbed the second Battle of Britain for Celtic, saw Liverpool travel to Parkhead on 13 March with Michael Owen, Steven Gerrard, Emile Heskey and co all sensing a place in the last four of the competition. Celtic, however, were buoyed by the return of Henrik Larsson, who at one stage looked likely to miss the remainder of the league season. The inspirational striker returned to partner John Hartson up front. Celtic had notched up an impressive nine consecutive wins on home soil prior to the match, but O'Neill admitted such a record would count for nothing with Liverpool in town. 'Our home record won't help us a jot,' he told the *Mail on Sunday*. 'We are capable of losing, too. Don't get me wrong: it is a terrific record. Every game we have played in recent Euro matches has been exhilarating. I actually prefer to play away from home first, even though winning the first leg at Parkhead has become vital to our recent progress. Last season, away against FC Porto and Rosenborg in the Champions League, we seemed to find scoring a problem – but this season we have scored two at Blackburn and Stuttgart and one against Celta Vigo. You can lose to any team in European football and as soon as Liverpool found themselves out of the Champions League they were among the favourites to win the UEFA Cup. You know their style of play because you have seen it so often. Even Johan Mjallby, for example, told me he grew up watching English football every week in Sweden. There are less surprises because you know the players well – I didn't know much at all about Celta Vigo. It is alright looking at videos and I even watched them on numerous occasions, but it is still a trip into the relative unknown. Lazio would have been exciting because they are a new side, but the TV audience and money would not have been the same. There is also the Battle of Britain element – if someone had told me after the Basle defeat that we would get Liverpool in the UEFA Cup quarter-finals then I would have taken it. I am not sure how Liverpool will approach the game. The year they won the tournament, they were a brilliant counter-attacking side. Their pace made it impossible to invite teams to come at them.'

After the disastrous preparations for the Stuttgart tie, Celtic supporters were delighted to see their side beat Rangers 1-0 in the league match before the Liverpool tie – the ideal preparation for a massive European night at Parkhead. O'Neill said: 'The Liverpool game is a separate tournament and a separate set of circumstances. However, it is better for us to go into the game having beaten Rangers than having lost.' Liverpool boss Gerard Houllier spoke of his admiration for the Bhoys. 'Celtic are a strong side and very consistent,' he told the *Daily Post*. 'They are a huge club with a huge base of fans as well. They played extremely well when they faced Blackburn earlier in the UEFA Cup and the three wins they had against Blackburn, Celta Vigo and Stuttgart were impressive.'

Speaking of O'Neill's personal record against the Merseyside club, Houllier added: 'Martin is a clever guy and, yes, he had a good record against us when he was manager at Leicester. One game was played on the back of a Worthington Cup final when we had just beaten Birmingham – so I have got a lot of respect for him and also for his team. We take every team in this competition with great respect and concentration. But we are not scared whatever the record of the past or the atmosphere. Whatever people say, whatever the history, it is the game that matters. They have got a very good record in Europe and in the Scottish League and they should have been with us in the Champions League, they were very unlucky not to qualify.'

Predictably, Larsson got Celtic off to a dream start inside

three minutes, only for O'Neill's former charge Emily Heskey to equalise a quarter of an hour later. That was the way it stayed for the rest of the game to hand Liverpool a real advantage in the tie. A clean sheet at Anfield would be enough to send Houllier's men through. The match, however, was overshadowed by a disgusting act by Reds forward El Hadji Diouf, who spat at a Celtic fan, to widespread condemnation. Houllier told the *Express*: 'We view the matter extremely seriously – the player has apologised for his reaction. No matter what the provocation, he should not have reacted the way he did. It is not conduct we consider acceptable for a Liverpool player. He is a young player and I may forgive him because he felt he had been hit by a fan, but I cannot accept his actions. He spoiled the game for us.'

O'Neill, meanwhile, said he did not see the incident but added: 'We got a goal, but I was disappointed with the equaliser. Liverpool came here to get a goal and proved themselves by counter-attacking. They knocked the stuffing out of us for a spell, but we are still in with a chance. We are enjoying the limelight and big matches.' He told the *Daily Record*: 'We are still in the tie without a doubt. I don't want to go out of the UEFA Cup without having had a go. We are capable of scoring at Anfield and it looks as if we are going to have to win there. Why not? We might as well have a go at it.'

Diouf's actions earned him a two-match ban, meaning he would miss the return leg at Anfield. O'Neill commented: 'I have not actually seen the incident, but I know Houllier has and he has apologised for it. Spitting is not a clever thing to do – there is no decorum about it. I know people were rightly angry about it and the incident marred a great occasion, but I have no concerns about the Celtic fans going south for the return. The fans are always good and we had 10,000 down at Blackburn for the game there earlier this season and everything seemed fine.'

On a European night, Anfield is one of the most intimidating and famous atmospheres in world football. Scarf-waving, vocal Liverpudlians singing in unison is enough to raise the hairs on the back of anyone's neck. Some of the biggest and best teams in the world have been rolled over on Merseyside, but on their grand tour of the 2002/03 season, Martin O'Neill's Celtic would not be one of them. Alan Thompson and John Hartson hit a goal apiece without reply to cap one of the best ever results for Celtic in European competition. O'Neill was delighted by the performance. After the game he said it proved Scottish clubs could compete with their more glamorous neighbours south of the border should Celtic and Rangers ever join the Premier League: 'It is a great night for us to beat a club like Liverpool on their own territory. It is an immense performance by the players. We have beaten Blackburn Rovers and we have beaten Liverpool here. I am sure anyone that was looking at it would feel we wouldn't disgrace the league if it ever happened. At the time when we played Blackburn there was a lot of talk about Celtic and Rangers going into the league. I felt then we were a team under pressure because, although Blackburn had just gone to Highbury and beaten Arsenal, I felt people would say it was only Blackburn. Well, if it was to materialise, we certainly showed Celtic would not disgrace the league.' Beaten Liverpool boss Houllier admitted Celtic played with a higher energy and would go into the semi-finals having claimed a massive scalp.

O'Neill was aware Euro glory would see his name alongside the greats of Celtic Football Club. He told the *Sunday Mail*: 'Gerard Houllier won the UEFA Cup with Liverpool two years ago and told me it gave him tremendous satisfaction as a manager to win a European trophy. It really is big, big news to win one. Not many people in football are fortunate enough to do it and now we are close. We are one of only four teams left and it might be as close as we get. We have had some fantastic results this season and I wasn't entirely sure if people around Europe were sitting up and taking notice. However, beating Liverpool 2-0 on their own ground to knock them out of Europe will prompt people to look at us in a different light. Our victories in Europe have given us confidence and when I see the likes of Ajax, Valencia and Juventus in the quarter-finals of the Champions League we can take some sort of reflected glory. Of course, it would be great to be in the Champions League next season and do something there, but we are happy with the way things are. In fact, I am ecstatic about what we have achieved in the UEFA Cup. I am really proud of my men and the result was remarkable. Every one of them was superb and, sometimes, I wonder where they get their energy from. To come out of the two-week period with games against Rangers and Liverpool and finish it with a result and performance like that is fantastic.'

While O'Neill had afforded himself the luxury of talking

about European success for the first time in the campaign, Celtic chairman Brian Quinn responded by singing the praises of his manager. He said: 'Martin has assembled a marvellous team, a great team. I don't see why we can't go all the way, we certainly have the quality to win it. The manager gets the best out of the players and makes sure they are determined and organised – the signs of real leadership. It is only natural he will want to bring in new faces, but the last time I looked the transfer market was closed until June. We have always supported Martin as best we can and will continue to do that to keep the club moving forward and making sure we remain successful.'

Though they had only lost twice in the league going into April, Celtic had drawn too many for O'Neill's liking and were held at Dundee on 6 April to hand the initiative back to Rangers, who were amassing a strong lead in the SPL with Celtic now holding two games in hand. Alex McLeish's side moved eight points clear as Celtic prepared for their semi-final clash. With one final Old Firm game remaining – one final chance to take points off their bitter rivals – nothing less than maximum points would be acceptable for the Celtic faithful.

Back on the European trail, Boavista, a solid Portuguese side from the city of Porto, now stood between O'Neill's Celtic and a place in the UEFA Cup final. While lacking the technical flair of Sporting Lisbon, Benfica or Porto themselves, Boavista had negotiated some tricky ties and proved themselves a force on home soil in their progress to the last four. 'Boavista reached the second stage of the Champions League last year, so they will command plenty of respect,' O'Neill told *The Times*. 'But I think we will get a bit of respect too, especially after winning at Anfield.'

Celtic may have performed badly in that season's domestic cups – losing out to Rangers in the final of the Scottish League Cup and to Inverness CT in the quarter-finals of the Scottish Cup – but, for O'Neill, it merely highlighted the fact that Celtic did not have a big enough squad to be able to compete on all fronts. He told *Celtic View*: 'If I draw one crumb of comfort from the cup defeat [to Inverness] it's that the scheduling would have left us unable to cope with the rest of the season. I would have taken a replay, but, I don't care what anyone says, it was just asking too much. The squad is simply not strong enough. I have to throw a bit of realism in. Put it this way, if you had said to me I would have to forfeit the Scottish Cup for the UEFA Cup, I would definitely have taken it.'

The media mudslinging ahead of the crunch semi-final began in earnest, with Boavista goalkeeper Ricardo stoking the flames by labelling the Bhoys a one-man team. 'Celtic depend excessively on Larsson,' he told the *Sunday Mail*. 'The match will be determined by how well we handle him, but we have prepared a special system so it should be OK. Our defence is great and they will find it hard to get past me. Playing in Glasgow first gives us an advantage, but it is vital every player gives 120 per cent. It's the most important match in our history. This year, we will arrive in the final, I am sure of that. Yes, Larsson is a great striker, but he isn't God. Strikers from Brazil are the best anywhere in the world – Swedish strikers aren't even the best in Europe. Larsson is just an individual, Boavista are a team. Celtic are favourites, but we are dangerous on the counter-attack. The UEFA Cup final will be between Boavista and Porto, I am sure of that.'

Refusing to get drawn into a war of words with the Portuguese, O'Neill preferred to reflect on the fickle nature of football and how his side would achieve nothing by falling at the penultimate stage. He said: 'It is funny how short memories can be. If we don't get past the semi-finals no one will remember our achievements in Europe this season. Maybe that is just me being cynical, but we have shocked a few people. Celta Vigo, for example, thought they would overwhelm us in the second leg in Spain. They had not scored in Glasgow, but that didn't matter. I know this because I spoke to people who were in and around their hotel. I am sure Vigo would have had decent respect for a Liverpool or a Manchester United, but they thought they were so much better than us.'

O'Neill's animated antics on the touchline may have earned him just the one touchline ban in Europe, but it was not a recent addition to his managerial style. Neil Lennon recalled an incident during their time at Leicester City. 'It was against Middlesbrough and Emile Heskey ran through on goal and hit the post,' he told the *Sunday Mail*. 'The gaffer was so engrossed he ran along the touchline following the run. He was leaping about, but he had gone so far he turned around and found himself in the 'Boro dugout!'

O'Neill admitted his touchline antics often had his daughters cowering behind the sofa. He added: 'My daughters Alana and Aisling tell me to cut out the jumping around on the touchline. There are times when I embarrass them and my wife Geraldine. When I see it later I might cringe. Although I don't feel it when I am involved in the game and doing it.'

O'Neill sensed Celtic were becoming a force away from home, and the 'travel sickness' that had plagued the side in European competition was a thing of the past. He learned this from the Liverpool game, where his squad had stood firm in the face of the famous Kop and had returned to Scotland with a victory. Now that they were down to the final four, O'Neill believed any one of them could win. 'I don't care whether you are two or 105, I don't think you can play the game without a nervousness,' he said. 'That keys you up. Now, if you are overwhelmed by it, that is a different matter and you shouldn't bother becoming a professional player. Substitute keyed-up for nervous and it comes down to the same thing. You are apprehensive, worried about your own game, for a start, and your team. The sooner you get over all those things and get down to play the better, and that will be it. But you can't relax in these matches, which are of such high intensity.'

Expectations were now suffocating at Parkhead. The side may have suffered some mishaps on the domestic front, but success in the UEFA Cup had become a realistic opportunity. 'We are getting ahead of ourselves,' O'Neill told the *Morning Express*. 'We are in the semi-final of the UEFA Cup and we will be going for it. This club is steeped in history and Jock Stein was a great manager – and the Lisbon Lions were a great team in 1967, as were the team who got to the final in 1970. So these were great days and they have not been around for some considerable time. Another victory would not diminish those days and it is up to us to try to have some success of our own. This club will always be steeped in history and you have to remember that is has been a long time since we were in Europe after Christmas.'

O'Neill was aware that big European semi-finals did not come around too often, and that the fact Celtic had knocked out Liverpool in the previous round did not necessarily make them favourites for the semi-final clash against Boavista. He had a few choice words for his squad. 'We have some older players who realise just what an opportunity this is. We may also have some younger players who think this sort of thing happens all the time. It doesn't – so make the most of it now. The players will be very nervous at the start and I assume the opposition will be too. But there is not a lot I will be able to do to calm them down because I will probably be in a worse state!'

The game itself, on 10 April, was a typically tense affair. A goalless slog from both teams at Parkhead came to an abrupt end when Joos Valgaeren put through his own net only for Henrik Larsson to make amends at the other end a minute later. Celtic's star striker then missed a penalty, which left the Bhoys needing a goal in Portugal to stay in the competition. O'Neill, though, maintained he was satisfied at half-time in the tie. 'The players are disappointed and a bit frustrated, but I am not,' he said. 'I think they are capable of going to Portugal and winning against Boavista. That is not just bravado. I think we can score and still go through.'

Some sections of the Parkhead crowd had jeered the

home side after the match, something that baffled the Hoops boss. He continued: 'My players were brilliant to beat the likes of Liverpool and Stuttgart in the UEFA Cup and were all looking forward to the semi-final at Celtic Park in front of their own supporters. Then some of our fans booed one of their own players when he played the ball back. The boos were prolonged and the player had actually played very well in the first half. If we had been beaten 12-0 it might just have been understandable that someone might have heckled in a UEFA Cup semi-final. But I told my players to take it as a backhanded compliment because it shows just how much we have raised the level of expectation. John Clark told me the Celtic crowd never booed the 1976 team.'

With the second leg getting closer, many could have forgiven the Celtic players for letting nerves get the better of them, something O'Neill had warned against, but the Bhoys had continued winning in the SPL and were finding form at the right time.

The return leg, on 24 April, was a glorious occasion for Celtic, who left it late to snatch a 1-0 win over the Portuguese side. Henrik Larsson netted the winner ten minutes from time to secure a 2-1 aggregate victory. It was far from a classic, as these high-stakes matches seldom are, but it was enough for O'Neill. 'It is fantastic – a really great feeling,' he said. 'I am delighted for everyone at the club, the players and the supporters – to be perfectly honest the only people we could hear were our supporters.'

Martin's wife, Geraldine, could not stand the tension and stayed at home, but both his daughters attended. He was delighted to share this occasion with his family and drew on comparisons with his days at Forest. 'Somebody asked me how this compares to getting to European finals as a player – but that was so long ago I can't remember how it felt,' he admitted, 'But obviously this is a terrific feeling to be taking Celtic to a UEFA Cup final. That is the best description I can give you at the minute. The goal was a long time coming, but we got there in the end. Obviously I was concerned because I was hoping we might create more chances during the game and we had also spurned one early in the first half. I always felt we would get a goal, but time was certainly running out and Boavista were dropping back in numbers and defending well. But if you go back over the games we have played to get to the semi-final then we really didn't want to go out with a whimper; that was the last thing we wanted so we tried to create chances, but it was wearing on the heart without a doubt. Then, when we did score, Boavista upped the tempo and, all of a sudden, there were balls coming in at us from all over the place. It was very tense for me. In fact, I can't remember being quite so nervous since my old days going to the discotheque when I had to explain why I was getting home at three in the morning – that was just as stressful.'

While a place in the UEFA Cup final had been secured, the SPL campaign was reaching a nail-biting climax with Celtic and Rangers slugging it out. It was all the more energy sapping for the Bhoys, who were drained from the European exertions. But as the season moved into May Celtic midfielder Neil Lennon was at the centre of an alarming incident. Following a routine win over

Motherwell, the Northern Irish midfielder was attacked by three men in Glasgow, suffering a cut lip as a result of the unprovoked attack. Martin O'Neill was no stranger to abuse in Scotland, with sectarian thugs launching a small number of alarming attacks on the Ulsterman. Lennon was insistent that he would not be driven south of the border in the face of these attacks. O'Neill admitted Lennon had endured a tough time since making the move to Celtic, though he had been a huge hit on the pitch for O'Neill's side.

If their European tour had been a grand trek through some of the continents greatest cities, brought to life by free-flowing football and tactical nous, then the final few months of the league campaign had become a long, hard slog. Ahead of their biggest game in a quarter of a century Celtic were also within touching distance of the league title. Before travelling to the UEFA Cup final, Celtic and Rangers were neck and neck, on 94 points and each with a goal difference of 68. It could not have been closer.

Celtic would face another Portuguese side, Porto, in the Seville showpiece after their comfortable 4-1 aggregate win over Lazio.

It was clear that O'Neill felt Celtic should have been in the Champions League this season, with defeat to Basel still smarting, but regardless of the outcome in Seville, it had been a marvellous season for Celtic. Victory would certainly put him up there with the greatest Celtic managers, if not the whole of Britain, among such esteemed company as Jock Stein and Brian Clough. 'We want to live for the moment,' he told the *Daily Record*. 'My reputation doesn't come into it. This is about making the most of an opportunity and it's important the players realise that. European finals don't come along every day. I know they are capable of doing this.'

The match, on 21 May, took place in the baking-hot city of Seville, which had been taken over by an army of Celtic supporters. Unlike most ordinary cup finals, where tension takes over and free-flowing football is at a premium, Celtic and Porto put on an incredible show for the gathered crowd, a sea of green and white. Derlei had put Porto ahead on the stroke of half-time, but a Henrik Larsson goal in the 47th minute levelled proceedings. The Swede struck again just short of the hour mark, after Dmitri Alenichev had restored Porto's slender advantage. The game went into extra-time and was destined for penalties, when Porto scored a precious third and hung on to win the game. It was heartbreaking for Celtic.

But after a spate of bitter incidents over the course of the season, there was one more for O'Neill to contend with due to the actions of the Porto players – who were guilty of time-wasting throughout the match. 'I know I will get into a lot of trouble, but it was poor sportsmanship at the end of the day,' he fumed. 'I wasn't pleased with it at all. They are very talented footballers and I am afraid I was not pleased. It has been a wonderful experience and the crowd were absolutely fantastic. The players put absolutely everything into the game and I couldn't ask for more. We came roaring back each time they scored, but I fancied us.'

The Celtic fans were angry at the way the match had panned out and vented their frustration at the Porto players. 'You saw the reception they got from our fans when they collected their medals and my own view is that Celtic have as fair-minded fans as there are in European matches and you saw their reaction,' he told the *Mirror*. 'Lots of things were going on there, but it doesn't matter now, it's gone.' O'Neill admitted he would always retain fond memories of the 2002/03 season, despite the bitterly disappointing end. 'I cant imagine we will feel the same heartbreak again,' O'Neill said. 'We won the treble in my first season and the league last year, but this is the most memorable season I can imagine. These things don't come around often and I want to be wrong, but it might be a few years before a Scottish club contests a European final again. I just know that the effort, determination and ability was incredible.'

There was one more mighty effort needed by Martin O'Neill and Celtic, who would need to pick themselves up from their European heartache to win the title. Celtic travelled to Kilmarnock needing to outscore Rangers, or they would finish the season empty handed. Though the Bhoys won the match 4-0, Rangers swept aside Dunfermline 6-1 to claim the title on goal difference – by a margin of just one goal – with both sides finishing on 97 points. It was another devastating blow to O'Neill, who took enormous pride in claiming the Championship. In the end, Celtic were beaten by the slenderest of margins and Rangers were celebrating their 50th league title.

It was heartbreaking for O'Neill, who struggled to find any positives at the end of a week of high drama. 'The team have played superb all season,' he said. 'We carried the SPL flag in a European final and coming back here to play in the championship games as well to carry right through to the final day. The effort they put in was magnificent, especially after playing in temperatures of 110 degrees, but defeat is always hard to take. We were a credit to Scottish football and Scotland should be proud of us.'

The grand European adventure had come to an end, but Celtic had proved themselves as a force in European football. The Champions League was O'Neill's next biggest challenge.

CHAPTER 8

DOMESTIC GLORY

'My high and low with Celtic came within the same evening.
Driving up to the stadium in Seville and seeing a sea of green and
white shirts inside. Those were amazing scenes. We had 80,000 fans
in the city, most of whom knew they would never get a ticket.
The disappointment was to lose the game in the fashion we did,
with a late goal from Porto in extra-time.'

O'Neill admitted he was worried about fatigue after what had been a long and gruelling 2002/03 season. He believed his pre-season schedule would need to be less demanding on the squad following their exertions the previous year. He told the *Daily Mirror*: 'It seems like five minutes ago that we were in Seville. Results are never important at this stage of the season, it's all just about getting the lads back into it, but, of course, it's nice to get a win. When we eventually get everyone together we'll start to step it up a bit. We played sixty games last year and it's not as if the players will have lost a phenomenal amount of fitness. They'll have lost a lot of match sharpness, but it's just a matter of dealing with it properly. Some of the older lads take a little bit longer to get into it, while the young boys absorb the heavier stuff easier. It's just a case of getting as much fitness work done as possible and, of course, steering clear of injury. The players are in the position where they know what I want from pre-season, and I know what they want. If you know players quite well you know their own habits and what they like to do and you know that their fitness will come up to the standard you expect.'

He was aware that Celtic's incredible UEFA Cup run had done more than raise the club's profile: it helped keep the flame alive for one of his key players. Neil Lennon had suffered more than most at the hands of sectarian thugs and O'Neill told the *Glasgow Daily Record*: 'Neil was a bit shaken by the incident after the Motherwell game and may have asked himself whether it was all worth it. When you combine that with the death threat and such things, he maybe weighed up everything and wondered what he would do. But I suppose, because of our UEFA Cup run, his mind was probably just on the football. I'm afraid this is something you have to live with. I believe there was an incident a couple of days ago with some of the Rangers players. Time is a bit of a healer and until it rears its head again you're inclined to forget about it and just get on with things. At the minute, he hasn't mentioned it, so I presume he's alright with things at the moment. There is always some thought that the things happening to Neil would make him want to head back south, but I don't think that is in his thoughts and that has been helped by the UEFA Cup final. Neil has been terrific for the club, a great influence – on the field anyway. There have been a couple of things off the field that, in retrospect, he may have thought about handling differently. But overall his performances have been excellent. I'm sure that when he stepped up from Leicester the idea of playing in Europe would have appealed to him, as would playing for Celtic. And probably in his wildest dreams he never thought he would have played in a UEFA Cup final.'

Celtic had the added bonus of a Champions League place, despite only finishing second in the league, but would need to negotiate two qualifying rounds in order to make the lucrative group stages of the competition. Their first opponents were Lithuanian side FBK Kaunas. Shortly before the tie, Kaunas striker Audrius Slekys was tragically killed in a car accident and, at O'Neill's behest, the squad and backroom staff pitched in to support the twenty-eight-year-old's widow. He said: 'It's very unfortunate for everyone here and all our sympathy goes to his family. If the club had wanted to postpone, we would have gone along with that. Because there is just a week between the two legs, I don't know if they could have postponed it. Under normal circumstances, I'm sure it would have been.' A thoroughly professional 5-0 win over two legs saw Celtic move one step closer to the main draw.

An exodus of players at Ibrox left many Celtic fans confident they could wrestle the title away from their bitter rivals, but O'Neill had not enjoyed the best of success in the transfer market. He had earned a reputation as a manager capable of securing late deals to bolster his squad, but O'Neill admitted he was still looking for quality additions to the squad to help maintain European success at Parkhead. He told the *Sunday Mail*: 'We would like to have added to the squad, but have been unable to and I can't turn the clock back. We still have a few weeks. Regardless, if we get in the Champions League, at worst we'll have the UEFA Cup. Even domestically I want things sorted and I've got until the end of the month, but I hope that it's not a mad dash. Despite my reputation for eleventh-hour dealings, it's not the way I want to work. I would have preferred to have done something before now, but the next deadline might come around without us having added anyone. I want quality because I'm not satisfied. It was a terrific run in Europe last year and we went close in the league. The players did brilliantly and I couldn't have asked for more of them – but that's all history. The fact is we can improve a great deal. I could buy six squad players. They would play their quota and I'd be able to give some big names a rest – but that's not where I want to go. We need that at European level, as I know presently we are full out in those games.'

Qualification for the group stages would help attract bigger names to Celtic Park and O'Neill called on the club's upper echelons to loosen the purse strings. Indeed, he believed he was paying for the mistakes of previous managers, who had attempted to buy their way out of trouble during Rangers' years of dominance prior to O'Neill taking the reins. 'Ideally, it would have been great to add to the squad, but I am not going to spend my time contradicting the chairman. If we are having to sell players before bringing players in, which is seemingly what he said, I wouldn't want to be trying to sell our best people in the next few days. It's not my job to read all the figures, but, if there are past debts to sort out, that would be a bit of disappointment as the manager. What has been said about money has not dampened my enthusiasm for the job I have with Celtic. We've had two really decent campaigns in European football in the last two seasons. The expectation is now very high and I have to manage that the best I can. We just have to get on with it and get some enjoyment from playing in the Champions League if we make it. If that's not good enough for the fans or other people, I can't do anything about that. I knew we weren't going to be looking at signing Juan Sebastian Veron, Damien Duff or Joe Cole, but I don't believe the effort in looking at players has been wasted. We played sixty games and all the major players missed parts of the season, including Henrik Larsson. John Hartson and Chris Sutton missed parts and you don't even realise people have missed chunks of the season, but we have to get on with it and hope we have enough players to cope. The last time we were in the Champions League we didn't field the same team two games running. That will probably be the case again. We just have to hope the main players stay fit for decent periods.'

MTK Hungaria stood between Celtic and a place in the Champions League proper and O'Neill admitted success in the competition was driving him at the time. He told the *Daily Record*: 'The Champions League has become the Holy Grail of European football. Everyone wants to be involved in it, from the players to the supporters, who just love it. I wouldn't be far behind that group myself. It is terrific and there is no doubt that during pre-season getting to the Champions League was uppermost in the thoughts of the players. We wanted to get through these qualifying games and while they came at an awkward time you had to get on with it. It's just the excitement of having six games in this fantastic competition. It should act as a spur that they want to repeat the experience of two years ago.'

A 4-0 win in Hungary, followed by a rather disappointing 1-0 victory at Parkhead, saw Celtic safely through to the group stages. A couple of big wins – particularly away from home – would have delighted their manager. However, the draw for the group stages pitted Celtic against Lyon, Bayern Munich and Anderlecht – three clubs with Champions League pedigree who would prove a real test for the Bhoys. For the first time since the Champions League took on its new name both Celtic and Rangers had made it through to the group stages. O'Neill hoped the standing of Scottish football, and greater attention from UEFA, would improve as a result. He commented: 'It's a great night for Scottish football. It is splendid and I'm delighted with events tonight. For the first time since the competition took a new name, there will be two Scottish teams there. We'll have six games to see how we get on. From a footballing point of view, it is just great to be there. The co-efficient has improved with these results. And if the national side – with a bit of luck – could even make the play-offs, it would be terrific.'

The domestic season had began with a goalless draw against Dunfermline, not the dream start for Celtic, but they soon found their stride, hitting five against Dundee United and Livingston before the Champions League returned in September.

While accepting Bayern Munich would be favourites to win the group, O'Neill admitted the three remaining teams would fancy their chances of securing second spot. He told the *Irish News*: 'I am absolutely delighted to be in it. It is a good draw for us and I am sure that Anderlecht and Lyon will be thinking the same way as us: that they can challenge for the second place. Geographically speaking, it is also a good draw for us with not too much travelling involved. Bayern Munich are one of the great European teams with fantastic pedigree in the tournament and I'm sure the group stages will give rise to some magnificent evenings here at Celtic Park. They are hard games for us, no doubt about it, but we are all looking forward to them. The draw brought back memories for me of two years ago when we were in the competition for the first time and I hope we can replicate that kind of form.'

A narrow 2-1 defeat to Bayern Munich in the group's toughest game – a trip to Munich's Olympic Stadium – was not a disaster for Celtic, who competed well against their illustrious opponents, and a brilliant performance at Parkhead saw the Bhoys stroll past Lyon 2-0.

In the league as well Celtic were proving all but unbeatable, with young midfielder Liam Miller earning high praise for his performances. October brought with it the first Old Firm clash of the season, which Celtic won courtesy of a Zurab Khizanishvili own-goal. All looked bright for O'Neill's Celtic, who had picked up maximum points after their draw on the opening day of the season. Dundee United and Livingstone had been put to the sword with ruthless five-goal defeats. But, disappointingly, their European campaign was about to hit the rails.

Anderlecht, who had plenty of Champions League experience, were certainly seen as beatable, but a 1-0 defeat in Belgium left the group wide open. The squad responded terrifically to sweep the Belgians aside 3-1 at Parkhead and were able to hold Bayern Munich to a goalless draw. It meant Celtic's future in the competition would be settled in the group's final match, against Lyon, on 10 December. O'Neill's side, who had not yet taken a point on their travels in the competition, would need at least one to make it through to the last sixteen.

The match may not have started well for the Bhoys – they fell behind to a Geovanni Elber goal after just six minutes – but they responded well and equalised courtesy of John Hartson's 24th-minute strike. Juninho Pernumbucano restored the home side's advantage just after half-time, but Celtic again rallied and, with a quarter-of-an-hour remaining, restored parity. Chris Sutton popped up with a goal to delight the travelling fans. It looked like Celtic would be able to hold out for a draw and the point they needed to progress, but late drama proved the undoing of O'Neill's team. Juninho dispatched a controversial penalty four minutes from time to break Celtic hearts. Bobo Balde was punished for an innocuous looking handball, but the referee awarded a penalty, much to the frustration of O'Neill. 'You can't give a referee any possibility of pointing to the spot and raising an arm is a dangerous thing. But it was not a deliberate handball. You tell me the rules of the game. All the Lyon players turned away. None appealed. It was a massive game and that was a massive decision.' One crumb of comfort for O'Neill came in the form of the UEFA Cup, a competition his squad were most familiar with. Finishing third in the group meant defeat did not signal the end of European competition.

In the SPL, Celtic continued to dominate and were scoring freely. Henrik Larsson was scoring for fun and the Bhoy's defensive solidity had returned. Teams were struggling to break Celtic down and they were threatening to run away with the league once again. Indeed in their first match of 2004 Celtic hosted Rangers knowing defeat would deliver another body blow to their title rivals. O'Neill was looking for three points but got much more, with a three-goal defeat deflating the struggling Rangers squad.

European football returned in February with a potential banana skin in the form of The Czech Republic's Teplice, but they failed to trip-up O'Neill's clinical Bhoys, a 3-1 aggregate win ensuring a plum fourth-round tie with European giants Barcelona. Celtic, under their current boss, had been known to cause a few upsets in European competition, but ties did not come any harder than the Catalans, who boasted the enigmatic Ronaldinho among their ranks. O'Neill mused upon the strides his side had made. He told the *Sunday Mail*: 'Considering we had to play qualifiers when I first arrived we have made some sort of progress. Generally I would have thought it would have taken us longer to get this far. We have been put to the test on lots of occasions and the lads have never stopped surprising me with their performances and results. A few stick out in my mind. The night we beat Juve in Glasgow was special and against Valencia at Parkhead was special even though we lost on penalties. Against Blackburn it was important for ourselves and the credibility of the SPL to win. They passed us off the pitch for 20 minutes or so and then disparaging remarks started appearing. So it was gratifying for us to beat them home and away. It gave the SPL respectability and gave us confidence. Then we ended up facing Liverpool, a team of high quality, and the odds were stacked against us, but we managed to do it.'

Frank Rijkaard's side, disappointed though they must have been to be competing in the UEFA Cup following a premature Champions League exit, travelled to Celtic Park in early March fancied as being among the favourites to win the competition. O'Neill had always been keen for his squad to show no fear and it was obvious he relished the match. 'We all perked up when we heard the draw,' he told *The Times*. 'Barcelona are a major attraction. Playing at the Nou Camp will be wonderful for my players. It is a wonderful stadium and I hope it will invigorate us. Ironically, we have done better away from home in the UEFA Cup than the Champions League, so I hope that continues.'

O'Neill admitted he was mesmerised by Ronaldinho, who was beginning to fulfil his potential as the best player in the world. But before a famous trip to the Catalan capital, there was the game at Parkhead, itself an imposing stadium where few European teams fancy playing.

A second-half strike from Alan Thompson secured a famous victory for the Bhoys, one of the biggest of O'Neill's managerial career. It was a terrific win for Celtic, who were able to raise their game against the continent's biggest sides. They held a slender advantage, and O'Neill was aware that Barcelona could turn over more experienced teams on their own turf. But with three league games to be played before the return leg, he feared burnout in his squad. The Celtic manager was aware that protecting a one-goal lead in the Camp Nou would be a difficult job, but in the lead-up to the return leg, Celtic showed good form in picking up seven points from a possible nine to keep their league challenge on course. They held a 19-point advantage at the top of the table over a struggling Rangers side. But injuries were beginning to take their toll ahead of their biggest game of the season. The Camp Nou, a cathedral of world football, houses an expansive pitch that allows Barcelona to sweep teams aside with a brand of football unique to the club. It is very rare that they don't score on home turf, so it was widely recognised that Celtic's lead was a very fragile one. To make matters worse, following suspension to first-choice keeper Rab Douglas O'Neill was forced to blood nineteen-year-old keeper David Youngster in the match. The teenager did his manager proud, making a string of smart saves to keep out the blue and red tide, as Celtic secured an impressive 0-0 draw to progress to the quarter-finals. After the match, a delighted O'Neill said: 'I did have faith in David. I had said as much often enough. He made some terrific saves, one of them a touch over the bar in the second half that was wonderful. I said the day before the match that we would have to score and I really never thought for one moment the one goal we got at Celtic Park would be enough. I thought we would have to score and I am delighted to have been proved wrong. Barcelona are an excellent team and, of course, I was concerned about playing here. I thought Barcelona would score and I believed we had to as well. They put us under ferocious pressure and I expected that.'

Just days after a draining performance at the Nou Camp, O'Neill's Celtic travelled to Ibrox for their most emotionally challenging trip of the season. With his squad at breaking point, it was testament to the spirit and will of the Celtic squad that they were able to pick up a 2-1 win at the home of their bitter rivals. It gave Celtic an almost insurmountable 19-point lead. It was effectively job done in the SPL. O'Neill though, was not about to let his players rest on their laurels. 'I did worry about them being weary beforehand and thought we would have to weather a heavy storm early on,' he told the *Daily Record*. 'But I was delighted to get the first goal. After that, Rangers came into the game and I was pleased to get in at half-time still a goal ahead. We scored the second and could have got a third or fourth, but Stefan Klos made a great save and at that stage we looked reasonably comfortable, though I never thought that would be possible. I knew tiredness would come into it. Rangers had to go for it and I felt those spurned chances could go against us. And I thought the game could turn in their favour if they got one back, but thankfully that goal came in the 82nd minute. These players have played a lot of games at a high tempo and now, for the first time, we will start to think about changing the side around for league games.'

It was a luxury O'Neill could afford, as it was possible for Celtic to tie up the league title within a week. But, having remained unbeaten in the league up until April, O'Neill's charges found themselves two-goals down to Hearts in a game that – had Rangers lost – would have crowned Celtic champions. The Celtic players, demonstrating the never-say-die attitude that had seen them sweep aside all in the SPL, scored twice in the final three minutes to level the match. A delighted O'Neill told the *Sunday Mail*: 'The Celtic players do it every week, give every ounce they have got, and the fans should be proud. I never even contemplated defeat, I always believed we have time and also that if we got one, we could get two goals. Our home record pushed us on. It is something we all want to preserve. But it is only called Fortress Celtic Park because the boys have put in such an incredible effort to make it happen.'

Celtic were rewarded for their win over Barcelona with a UEFA Cup quarter-final clash against, Villareal, with the first leg to be played at Celtic Park on 8 April. With the Spanish side boasting the likes of Javi Mari, Juan Roman Riquelme and Javi Venta among their stars, it was another tough draw for Celtic, but they acquitted themselves with distinction. Having fallen behind to Josico's eighth-minute effort, Celtic equalised in the second half through Henrik

Larsson. But the damage had already been done. The crucial away goal, which counts double, had given Villareal something tangible to hold on to on home soil.

A trip to El Madragal, Villareal's imposing, compact stadium proved too much for the battling Bhoys, who were undone by a goal in each half as they proved unable to repeat the glorious away days of recent years. While the Champions League may have been O'Neill's ultimate goal, the UEFA Cup matches had not only given him the opportunity to pit his wits against some strong European sides, they had also given him an opportunity to assess his team's shortcomings and he was in no doubt what was needed.

He told *The Times*: 'We have had four great years. Some [players], such as Chris Sutton and Alan Thompson, have pledged their future to the club, but we need to freshen things up. In the present climate of clubs going into administration we want to get a side together and go forward in the Champions League. I want to go into the competition with a realistic chance. I look at Arsenal and the players they have, like Thierry Henry and Patrick Vieira, and that is what I am trying to aspire to. We have 60,000 people every fortnight at Celtic Park, which makes us a big club, but that does not necessarily mean you have the same chances as others. I have a fair idea of the finances available to me. The next thing I have to think about is Henrik leaving. The side has been together for a couple of seasons and that is reflected in the number of games we have played. It is incredible to think that we have played thirty-one matches in European competition in the last two years. The disappointment in going out of the UEFA Cup this time at the quarter-final stage, after reaching the final last time, is great. We wanted it to be another Seville for the fans. It is good to come back after a disappointment in Europe. Winning the title puts us back in the Champions League. This team has done so well, it has coped with sixty games a season. When I was at Nottingham Forest, we won the European Cup by playing just nine games.'

The price of success in Europe in the 2002/03 season had been a runners-up spot in the SPL, something that hurt everyone associated with the club – though the road to Seville had been paved with golden moments. A year previously, a 4-0 thumping of Kilmarnock had not been enough to prevent Rangers from lifting the title and O'Neill was determined not to suffer a similar fate. He told the *Daily Record*: 'You don't get over these things in a couple of minutes. That evening in Kilmarnock was the time we all made our minds up that, if we could, we would avoid the same this season. Sometimes it takes a disappointment to bond people together. Setbacks such as that used to take me a long time to get over as a player but, as I get older, it takes a lot longer, believe me.' And he admitted it took until the start of the current season for the pain of Seville to ease. 'It was an incredibly exciting day but it is far more exciting when you are on the end of it,' he continued. 'Unfortunately we weren't. It took me all summer to get over it. It was not until we opened the new season against Dunfermline that I wasn't waking up in the morning and cursing our luck. Not only had the championship gone, but we knew we were going into a double set of qualifying games for the Champions League and we did not know who we were going to get. We also had a trip to America booked up. Commercially that was important for the club, but we realised we would have a long trip coming back and that we might have to go straight into a qualifier away from home, which was exactly how it turned out. There was always the fear that we could get knocked out of the competition before the new season had even started. I did not think we would be so dominant domestically this season. I thought it would be very, very tight for every reason under the sun, just as I expect it to be again next season. Will we win twenty-five consecutive games again next season? Absolutely no chance, not a prayer. That is why I have been so delightfully surprised this season because I did not think we would have a chance of going thirty-eight games unbeaten. But if you had said to me after our opening day draw at Dunfermline that our next twenty-five league games were going to be victories I would have had a decent bet with you on that one.'

Having wrapped up the title with consummate ease, O'Neill was able to rest some of his squad and devote more time to improving the side. Inspirational striker Henrik Larsson and young Irish midfielder Liam Miller were destined to leave the club at the end of the season, leaving O'Neill with a number of holes to fill. He told the *Daily Star*: 'We cannot go into the season with the squad the size it is. You have to pay for quality so it is a delicate situation in this financial climate. It is a fact that my old club Leicester City in the Premiership get somewhere between £16 million and £20 million a season from television money, whereas Rangers and ourselves have an absolute maximum of £1.5 million so we are a fair way down to start with. The difficulties of getting into the elite are obvious.'

In a documentary, O'Neill revealed the weight of expectation at Parkhead: 'Rangers had dominated Scottish football throughout the 1990s. So I could understand and talk about having a bit of battered pride and, perhaps over the past couple of seasons, we have restored that. With a bit of pride restored, you start to restore a bit of hope, then a bit of expectation and all of those snowball into a sort of delirium effect. Handling that is a bit of a concern. Two years ago, I thought it was a problem. Now I just have to get on with it. As long as you keep the dressing room pretty sane, the rest of the other things will take care of themselves. Football has changed in my thirty-odd years in the game. I thought there was probably more of a level playing field way back in Celtic's day and maybe Nottingham Forest's day in 1979/80. Now the power seems to be where the money is and that is a bit of a problem – but it doesn't stop me dreaming and having a go. By the end of this season, you go on maybe ten days' holiday or whatever the case may be, then you are back at it. And the season before, that is forgotten about.'

The 2003/04 campaign would be the last with the club for Celtic hero Henrik Larsson. The Swedish striker finally decided to call time on his Parkhead career and look for a new start elsewhere. There was no doubt that

Larsson had been the most consistent, professional and mesmerising footballer under O'Neill's tutelage and was someone who was always fondly remembered by the Ulsterman. Reflecting on the Swede's personal performance in the losing UEFA Cup final, he told the *Glasgow Daily Record*: 'I might have watched the game again if we had won. Maybe I'll have a look at it when I retire. What I don't need reminding of was the way Henrik worked that night. It was my personal highlight of his seven years at this club. Henrik has been brilliant and, of course, I am sad to see him go. Celtic had the foresight to take a chance on signing Henrik when clubs in England had either paid no attention to him while he was at Feyenoord or were still making up their minds about him as Celtic moved in. Either way, this club gambled and they have been repaid a hundred times over for having the courage of their convictions. Henrik was on his way back from the most serious injury of his career, the leg break he suffered against Lyon in the UEFA Cup when I became Celtic manager. I can still see his first game for me, against Dundee United at Tannadice in August 2000. He opened the scoring that day, bending the ball into the net with his left foot while he still had those dreadlocks blowing in the wind.'

Without Henrik Larsson, Chris Sutton and John Hartson would lead the attack for the Hoops. In the summer of 2004, O'Neill stayed behind as his squad travelled to the USA to take part in a series of glamorous friendlies against some elite European sides. His wife Geraldine's health had become a concern and O'Neill, rightly, was putting her well being first – though he was able to join the tour before its conclusion. He told the *Sunday Mirror*: 'Things were looking brighter for Geraldine and I thought it was important for me to get out and I joined up for the second half of the America trip. At that stage I hadn't any intention of doing anything other than carry on.'

Celtic's ageing squad, having lost the youthful, highly rated Liam Miller, lured south of the border to Manchester United, needed freshening up in order to compete in what O'Neill hoped would be a busy season both domestically and on the European stage. Celtic could have been forgiven for cursing their luck after being drawn in a Champions League group alongside European giants Barcelona and AC Milan, although they had got the better of the Catalan giants in the UEFA Cup during the previous season. The final team in the group was Shakhtar Donetsk, a team that would be no push over, with few clubs relishing the long trip out to Eastern Europe to play in the harsh conditions the Ukranians are so accustomed to.

A summer trip to the USA would see O'Neill's Celtic face off against Manchester United, Chelsea and Roma, all of whom have budgets far superior to Celtic and who gave O'Neill a glimpse of the financial muscle of England's Premiership teams. But the summer was far from ideal preparation for O'Neill, who told the *News of the World*: 'It would certainly be right to say it has been a more difficult summer than normal for me, absolutely. But, as I have said, I don't have a monopoly on bad news. It happens. It's a fact of life. While you think you are concentrating on work and looking at certain things, it has been a difficult time. I am not saying I didn't go to the European Championship for that one specific reason, but it was a part of it. However, it is now a matter of refocusing and refocusing pretty quickly. I think that is the most important thing to do now. Last season it was different because we came back from this same trip to the USA and had to go straight into an away qualifier in Lithuania for the Champions League. That was my concern about the whole trip before it happened and that was how it turned out.

'Thankfully we scored a couple of early goals out in Kaunas and it settled us down. This time we don't have that problem with the Champions League, but we do have a problem with the number of games in quick succession. As it stands at this time we have played four on the trot in America, so it is a matter of trying to balance that out. Liverpool have just spent £15 million on a centre-forward [Djibril Cissé] and by the time the season starts Chelsea will probably have spent another £35 million. We are competing in that market and that is the difficulty. Trying to get those types of players in and then competing in the Champions League is easier said than done. As for Rangers, you know my views. I never think there has been much between them and us. It is a new season and Rangers have decided to renew their team. They have made about six changes and got a little bit of pace in their side. They are physically bigger, too. Henrik is a big loss, but he would be a big loss to any club. It is up to us to replace him. To ask some of the younger lads to step up and take on that mantle early might be a difficult task, but that does not prevent us from knowing we need some replacements. It would be lovely to replace Henrik with another Henrik, but we always knew it was going to be difficult and that was when we had a year to prepare for it. It still won't get any easier when he actually goes. Age, to be honest, would not be the most important thing on my mind.'

'Celtic and Rangers are big clubs, but TV money is dictating a great deal,' he told the *Irish Times*. 'We get £1.2 million – teams that stay in the English Premiership get £25 million plus. That is a massive dent in us proceeding. Sometimes you look rather enviously at that. But money seems to follow money so, despite the great size of Celtic, despite the great support, we are in the wrong environment. At this minute in Scotland only Celtic and Rangers are capable of withstanding a season. On any given day you can lose, but at the end of the season either Rangers or Celtic will win the league. That was not the case before. With respect, the Scottish League is in poor shape; poor shape in the sense that thirty years ago Hearts, Hibs, Aberdeen and Dundee United were pretty strong. Does that leave you equipped to play European football? The answer is that if you are playing strong, competitive football every single week, then European football is not as demanding in terms of a leap. You become battle hardened. I mean, there are only so many sides that can win the English league, but the matches are tough every week. In Scotland the opposition do raise their game and the games are difficult. Don't respect that and you will get done. The environment in which we are involved does not give us the wherewithal. I understand Celtic looking prudently, but our debt is very manageable indeed. The problem is that you can manage debt, but expectation remains very high. Trying to manage that with the resources you have is the difficult thing and – occasionally – the frustrating thing. The frustration is not always present, but there is no doubt that at this minute, when you see what we have done domestically and in Europe, when you think of Seville and what a driving force that is to push on, the frustration is that, actually, to push on, you definitely need strength. Our squad, by comparison to other squads looking for the same in Europe, is just not there. The periphery here is just not good or strong enough.'

While domestic success perhaps came too easily for the Bhoys in the 2003/04 season, there was always the European stage to keep O'Neill and his more senior players more than interested. 'To me that is the crucial question of it all,' he told the *Sunday Herald*. 'Whether those players that you feel have the hunger to go and do it again, actually do. Whether that is there, only time will tell, but to me that is a crucial element of it all – whether they can go the course again. Also, the last thing that players want to read about is that their position is the one that I am looking to strengthen. Some of the major players here would like to help, a bit of reinforcement, they would welcome those things, especially with the loss of Henrik, but that is my job. I think that with the younger players like Beattie, McGeady, Wallace and people like that, even though they have got plenty of potential, to ask them to go and compete immediately at the big level of European football without actually getting their toes wet in the SPL is asking a lot.'

By the time Celtic's first Champions League game came around, the visit of Barcelona, the Bhoys had already won their first five league games, including the scalp of Rangers in the first Old Firm derby of the season. A 3-1 defeat to Barca was succeeded by a 3-1 defeat at the San Siro to Milan. Indeed it was November when Celtic first suffered a league defeat, at the hands of Rangers to make matters worse. Celtic's invincible title had finally slipped. 'Someone said a couple of weeks ago they would like to see me in a crisis,' he told the *Mirror*. 'You should have been at Leicester in those first few months. You don't know what crisis is. You think you come here and it is easy. If that was the case this club would not have had eight bosses in nine years. You can't just put your finger in something and it works. If I lose my job here for some reason or another it will be because I have not won enough matches. But I have not lost the plot, I will have lost the plot when I am not winning matches.'

In the Champions League, Celtic took their first points of the season with a home win over Shakhtar and managed to secure draws against the group's 'big two'. Following the draw at the Nou Camp, O'Neill told the *Daily Record*: 'We had world-class players playing against us and we were forced back because of the wonderful play of Barcelona. We had to defend and did it wonderfully.' However while a draw at the San Siro may have been commendable, it was not enough to save Celtic from

European oblivion, as they crashed out before Christmas and did not even have the solace of a UEFA Cup place for consolation; domestic competition was now all that remained for the Bhoys and even that would end in disappointment. Despite winning a game more than Rangers, Celtic's six defeats would come back to cost them dear as their bitter rivals took the SPL title by a point. Needing victory at Motherwell, Chris Sutton looked to have won the title for Celtic with a goal on the half-hour mark before a Scott McDonald brace in the final two minutes snatched the points – and with it the title – from Martin O'Neill's hands. Rangers did their job, and won at Hibernian courtesy of a Nacho Novo goal in a dramatic final day of the Scottish league season. It was desperately unfortunate for Celtic, who were made to rue a poor run of form. With three minutes remaining at Fir Pirk, the title was Celtic's. Football can be a cruel game and O'Neill's last league game proved one of his most heart breaking.

Still Celtic had the Scottish FA Cup to compete for and would face Dundee United in the final – in what would be O'Neill's last game in charge of Celtic. 'These are the best fans in the world – even if they do get a bit agitated if we are not 3-0 up at half-time,' he told the *Sunday People*.

It was while playing a youth match in County Derry that Martin O'Neill first laid eyes on Geraldine McGrath, then fifteen years old. A priest at church introduced them and within a week their thirty-five-year romance had begun. O'Neill would soon move to England with Nottingham Forest, but managed to keep the relationship going and the couple were married in 1979; ever since, Geraldine had been the focal point of his life. After missing the Scottish Cup final in 2004, rumours about her health began to surface and, in January 2005, O'Neill confirmed that his wife was been battling cancer. Opening a cancer unit at Belfast City Hospital at the time, he said: 'My own wife had lymphoma and she is recovering from that battle against it.'

On 25 May 2005, O'Neill announced that he would step down as Celtic boss at the end of the season to care for his wife. While the decision did not come as a shock to the football world, who knew O'Neill as a fiercely proud and loyal family member before all else, his departure was met with sorrow by the club. Chairman Brian Quinn led the tributes for the boss who had revolutionised the Parkhead side. 'Martin O'Neill's contribution to Celtic has been quite immense. He has played a central role in the club's enormous success over the past five seasons and he goes with sincere best wishes from everyone associated with the club. While it will come as a great disappointment that he is leaving, we fully respect the reasons behind his decision. He has continued working for the past 18 months despite great pressure on personal stress.'

It had been an 'honour and privilege' to serve the club and become part of Celtic's history and O'Neill was grateful to everyone at the club for some of the best years of his career. He spent 281 games at the helm of Celtic, winning 212, losing 40 and drawing 29 – a phenomenal record that would put him up there with the Parkhead greats. But O'Neill needed to be with his family at this time. He told the *Evening Times*: 'She [Geraldine] is someone who stood by me and I want to give her some time back. We got some good news last year, but not so this year. I never felt her illness was that imposing until recently. Now, she is not so clever. I felt my resignation was the correct thing to do. She would not want me to be mentioning her, but sometimes I think she deserves it. I take my courage from her. It is difficult, but as I have said before, I haven't any monopoly on bad times. Everybody has them and everybody copes.' As for Celtic, they wasted little time in bringing in Scottish manager Gordon Strachan to take the reins after O'Neill's departure. The Ulsterman made an emotional farewell to his players at the Scottish Cup final against Dundee at Hampden Park.

O'Neill understandably kept his thoughts close during this difficult time, particularly after getting the all-clear the year before. 'I did not know what courage was a year ago until I watched her,' he continued. 'I could hardly spell biopsy a year ago, but I can certainly spell it now. I take a bit of courage from her and it keeps me going. Geraldine was first diagnosed in February of last year. She had treatments and everything was going fine. She got the all-clear, but it has returned. We had suspicions in recent weeks and that has taken it to a different level. We have had some discussions for some weeks as we awaited certain biopsy results. I waited until we had confirmation of how things were before I could make a decision about Celtic. The board of directors here knew all about how things were and were delighted, like me, over the Christmas period, when it looked like things were fine.

The board have just been great with me. It actually took a lot of courage for me to tell her about my decision to leave Celtic – but I firmly believe it is the right thing for the football club. You are always hoping for events to overturn and you are always hoping to wake up and things are different but it has not been like that.'

Knowing he could be an influential fundraiser for cancer charities, O'Neill set about on a new challenge. The outgoing Celtic boss wanted to help improve Scotland's outdated system of screening and treating patients. 'If there is anything I can do, I will. We are a bit short in Scotland, as I have found out, with a lot of research. There used to be some antiquated machinery being used. But there are things I wouldn't mind looking at to do something. There are machines that can pick up cancer relatively quickly, but they cost something like one million. This is the sort of thing I could help with, and if I could do something I would be delighted.'

Peter Lawwell, Celtic's chief executive, had the final say: 'At the moment, it is all about his family. But I would like to thank Martin for his contribution to the club. Martin has already proved himself a legend at this club,' he said. 'He will take his place among the Celtic greats.'

CHAPTER 9

TRIUMPHANT RETURN

'If you had told me that we could finish in the top four this season but had to forsake the UEFA Cup – it is very obvious that is the route I would go down.'

B ill Shankly once famously said: 'Some people believe football is not a matter of life and death, but it is much more important than that'. Martin O'Neill proved how this was not the case when he took himself out of the game from May 2005 to August 2006 to take care of his wife Geraldine. 'I am going to have to disagree with Shanks,' O'Neill said on his return. 'I think I have got a broader perspective of life. I still have tunnel vision in terms of football, but it does not mean I am less enthused.'

O'Neill made no secret of his desire to take on the England job in the wake of Sven Goran Eriksson's departure after another quarter-final defeat in a major tournament – the 2006 Fifa World Cup in Germany – finally brought an end to the Swede's reign. The FA, though, opted for a period of continuity and employed

Steve McLaren, Eriksson's assistant, as the new boss of the national side. 'It's gone, you get over it,' O'Neill told *The Times*. 'It was a genuine honour to be on the shortlist. The FA made their decision, though if they were to look at it again, they probably should have left it until after the World Cup finals.' While England would struggle under McLaren, culminating in their disastrous failure to qualify for the 2008 European Championships in Austria and Switzerland, the Three Lions' loss would prove to be Aston Villa's gain.

Chairman 'Deadly' Doug Ellis had his man. Since finishing second in the the first-ever Premiership season in 1992/93 under Ron Atkinson, Aston Villa had flattered to deceive for a number of seasons – trailing off at the crucial stage after positive starts to the campaign. The top four in the Premier League had become more entrenched than ever, although the fact that Everton had been able to breach the exclusive club had given Aston Villa cause for optimism. O'Neill had been touted as the prime candidate for the Villa Park hotseat and, on 4 August 2006, news of his appointment was confirmed: Martin O'Neill was the new manager of Aston Villa Football Club.

At a press conference confirming his appointment, O'Neill admitted to being: 'Absolutely petrified. It is a fantastic challenge and I am willing and ready to go. I have a lot of enthusiasm, but I am ready. I want to do it. I think everyone is well aware of the history of the soccer club and trying to restore it to those fantastic glory days. It is nearly a quarter of a century ago from when it won a European Cup, though we are a long way from that. In just over a fortnight we play at Arsenal, so that's a fair baptism.'

Behind the scenes, the financial future of the club was still in turmoil. Club chairman Doug Ellis was consulting with a number of parties to buy out the club. However, in spite of the potential problems, the size of Aston Villa, the talent within the squad and the potential for future investment were major factors in O'Neill's decision to end his fifteen-month hiatus. Clearly delighted with the appointment, Villa fans gave a vociferous welcome to their new manager. O'Neill said he was overwhelmed by the greeting. 'I knew I had to take this job after Mr Ellis offered it to me because I am told that when I get interviewed for jobs, I don't get them. I didn't want to have to go through many more interviews.'

Doug Ellis was known for his ruthless nature with managers and said the size of the crowd greeting the Ulsterman was similar to those that had greeted Tommy Docherty and Ron Atkinson – two managers given the axe by Ellis – when they had joined the club. 'I am worried because I can recall what happened to those two managers,' O'Neill continued. 'I think I will have to walk down the corridor backwards on my way out! Every club with a great history wants to recapture those past glories and I would love to be the man who can bring silverware back to this club. There has rarely been a day during the last fifteen months when I haven't thought about going back into football.'

Ellis told of how he got O'Neill to sign for Villa. 'We had three meetings at my home and I told Martin that I was not talking to anyone else. There were a dozen other applicants, but I always wanted Martin to be the manager.' O'Neill responded sharply: 'The dozen applications were all from me. Some funds are available and I am going to use them. Every manager will say he needs to strengthen his side and I am the same. I have seen the players only from a distance and I don't think you know them until you are working with them on a daily basis. I had a brief conversation with a couple of supporters outside and it kind of worried me,' he continued. 'Expectations are pretty high. The best way for me to ingratiate myself to supporters is by winning a couple of games and if I lose then I know the consequences. I wasn't sure if anyone would be outside the ground when I turned up and I was rather taken aback. It is a one-year rolling contract, but that is not an issue at all. I sometimes worked on a handshake at Celtic with Mr Desmond and I have had three five-year spells at clubs during my managerial career. I had a six-month spell at Norwich and that is the only contract I have broken – and I am not best pleased with myself over that.'

If Villa fans were alarmed by the type of contract afforded to O'Neill, he insisted he would be calling the shots at Villa Park. 'I am one of the very few men in this life who is not under the thumb,' he told the *Sunday Express*. 'I very seldom ask my wife anything; she just has to follow. I know a lot of people in life who are very much under the thumb, but I am not one of them – I am stronger than that. I had no reservations about coming here and no apprehension about working with Mr Ellis. I didn't canvas anybody for their opinion about this job, but Ron Atkinson still told me the other day he thought the club was fantastic. And he was actually very complimentary about the chairman. But it would not have mattered what Ron had said because I have to make my own mind up about these things.'

He continued boldly: 'As of today I take ownership of the football team. I have to deal with whatever comes and goes. I will take full responsibility and I certainly won't be throwing up any excuses. It is such a fantastic old ground and you really do feel the history of the place. There is a wonderful picture in the corridors of Villa Park in 1907, when they were playing Liverpool, and it's just fantastic. From behind the goal, you can see where the stands have now been built and you can see the church, which is still there. The steps were not particularly steep and you wonder how everyone saw the game. And then there is all that other history, like Villa winning the European Cup.'

He told the *Mirror*: 'When I was unveiled I was kind of hungry after the proceedings. I went to have a quick look around Villa Park and it was getting late, so I asked the chairman if he could point me in the direction of the nearest restaurant. He did better than that; he came with me. It was a chat and a quick meal, nothing more than that. The meal was pleasant and it was on the chairman, he insisted on paying. My solicitor was with me; some Villa people were nearby and came over to see us. It turned into a nice little gathering. I got back home at 2am, and then I was up at four to catch a flight to Germany.'

At the time of O'Neill's appointment, Villa were a struggling club. They were not in disarray, but Aston

Villa's supposed fickle supporters were desperate for success and the current squad did not seem capable of achieving it. O'Neill accepted he would have to instil a sense of pride in some of the players, telling *The Times*: 'I hope the players retain some enthusiasm for playing for the club, even those who may be disenchanted. On a general basis I will try and persuade them to stay, but if I am unable to, if I can't convince them, I don't want to keep those who are unhappy. I will meet them individually, that is the best way. They may have a personal gripe or moan and I might be able to sort it out. There is no point in me saying that everyone is going to stay, but what I don't want is them walking out the door when I have not spoken to them.'

Off the pitch, the battle for control of Aston Villa intensified. American tycoon Randy Lerner looked favourite to buy the club, but an eleventh-hour bid from the 'AV06' consortium ensured things were less than clear cut in the West Midlands. Lerner's bid had been officially received and recommended. There were fears, which ultimately proved unfounded, that the new owners of the club would not want O'Neill as the manager of the football club. Fortunately, billionaire Lerner had already given his backing to O'Neill. Despite having been in the job barely a fortnight, O'Neill was being forced to comment on his future and boardroom battles before fully settling in to his new role. 'I have not agreed anything with any particular consortium, be it Mr Lerner or anyone else and he is obviously in pole position. I spoke to Mr Lerner beforehand and I think he would be happy to keep me on as manager of the football team, but outside that, nothing has been talked about, confirmed or agreed. It really is as simple as that. I came in under the current regime. I was obviously well aware of all the speculation and the possibilities of a takeover. I actually signed here to Aston Villa under Doug's reign. I don't think Villa have to worry too much about whether I will hang around or not. I think my record over the past fifteen years suggests that I am not going to be leaving after a couple of months, unless, of course, I am forced to.'

Speaking of the lack of time he had to prepare his Villa squad, O'Neill told the *Independent*: 'Ideally it would have been great to postpone the season for a few weeks, but that is the way it goes. I wanted to come to this club and time was running out, so you go for it. I can understand the excitement because everything has been condensed into a couple of weeks. I have got plenty to prove to myself and to the Aston Villa people, but I would not want it any other way. After the commotion surrounding my arrival here, there's a period when people say, "Let's see what you can do," and that's absolutely right. When I first came here I said something semi-jokey, semi-serious about being petrified, but I am actually really excited.'

Arsenal's new 60,000-seater Emirates Stadium would see its first action on the opening day of the 2006/07 season. Their first opponents, Aston Villa, would prove not be overawed by the occasion and snatched an impressive 1-1 draw. 'It was nice to be back,' O'Neill told the *Sunday Telegraph* after the match. 'I am still getting to know my players and I don't even know who the reserves are, but today I thought we were terrific. Overall I was very pleased.' However, spoiling Arsenal's house-warming party did not represent the grand sum of O'Neill's ambition for Aston Villa.

His first win came at Villa Park, in the first home match of the season, against Reading, who were looking to repeat their first-season success in the Premier League.

By September, Randy Lerner had won the battle for control at Aston Villa and it was hoped the billionaire American would inject some much-needed cash into the club. Chelsea had seen their coffers swelled considerably through foreign ownership and Villa fans were greedily eyeing Europe's top talent in the hope their new owner would splash out. For O'Neill, however, it was more important that the club's history and traditions remained in check. He told the *Sunday Mirror*: 'This is an English football club, steeped in history and tradition, and while everybody needs to move forward into a more progressive future, it should not mean you don't marry some of those attributes to tradition. I believe it is possible and I think that is what you want to do. The heritage of a football club is so important.' And in fact, although Lerner made it clear to O'Neill that he would not throw money at the club like Roman Abramovich had done at Chelsea, the end of Doug Ellis' reign at Villa gave cause for optimism.

In late September, O'Neill's Villa had earned praise for their performances, although turning draws into victories was proving difficult. Stalemates with Arsenal, Watford and West Ham took the shine off positive victories over

Newcastle, Charlton and Reading. However a trip to Chelsea would give O'Neill his first test against Jose Mourinho – the self-titled 'special one' – since the 2003 UEFA Cup final, which had seen the Portuguese manager get one over the Ulsterman. O'Neill commented in the *Sunday Mirror*: 'Brian Clough was arguably the greatest manager ever known and unquestionably the most charismatic. It would be hard to make comparisons with a man who was out on his own. I knew him and maybe didn't appreciate him all that at the time – especially when he gave me the No. 12 shirt! I think Mourinho has been a fantastic manager and, if his career finished now, he has won the European Cup and the Championship, but I am not sure I would make comparisons there – but that is only my viewpoint.'

Falling behind inside five minutes did not represent a dream start for the Ulsterman, but Gabriel Agbonlahor – fast becoming one of the best English strikers around – levelled to earn a hard-fought point at Stamford Bridge. After the match, O'Neill said: 'Jose came up to me at the end and said that I was contesting so many decisions that he feared I might be a candidate for a heart attack. He might have been right on both counts! In Seville it was him contesting all the decisions, so perhaps I got my own back.'

It had taken some time for Randy Lerner to speak out about Martin O'Neill, but, when he did, the talk was of a multi-million-pound deal to replace the rolling contract given to him by Doug Ellis. 'Martin O'Neill has got a great record and the history and the makings for a steady long-term commitment and that is the plan,' Lerner said. 'I want to focus on Martin now, even though I am just getting to know him, Martin is great.' A seven-game unbeaten streak at the start of the season had certainly endeared him to the Villa Park faithful, too.

Throughout his managerial career O'Neill had never been shy of public declarations of the need for investment in the team. At Aston Villa it would be no different. As January approached, and the transfer window reopened, O'Neill would have his first real crack at bringing in his own players to fit around the existing structure. General Charles Krulak, widely acknowledged as Randy Lerner's right-hand man, insisted changes were on the way at Villa. He told the *Birmingham Mail*: 'You never want to do anything in business that doesn't make a pound, but at the same time if you really opened up his [Lerner's] heart you would see it is claret and blue and he is here for more than just the business side. He is here because he loves Aston Villa and loves football. He went to school and university in England, he has lived here and so have I; we have had a deep love of English football and when this opportunity came it gave us a chance to get involved in a sport we are deeply in. We have got a real buzz. The reality is Villa has such a wonderful ethos and history about it and to have the opportunity to be a part of that and take it to the next step is very exciting for us. As the Americans say, "We are pumped". We are delighted to have O'Neill. Randy had a lot of conversations with Martin during the transaction and we could not be happier. He is more than just a brilliant manager and more than just a brilliant tactician.

He is a brilliant leader. What the Villa fans are seeing is not just a smart manager on the sideline, what they are seeing is a great leader who has taken a club and instilled within them a desire and a belief that they can do it, that they can win. He motivates in many ways. One, he just has an aura of success. Everything he has touched has been very good, but equally, if not more important, he inspires confidence in the players because he has confidence in them. They see that this man has confidence in their abilities and that brings forth great effort.'

It was clear O'Neill had made the right impression on the club's passionate owners, but for him it was crucial he was given backing in the transfer window. He told the *Daily Mail*: 'If you want to make a really decent fist of the job – and Randy Lerner wants to do that – then he knows we have to try and improve. He has told me that he knows this will take time. I am hoping I will get the victories to earn me that time. He has got a bit of belief that I can do it – and I hope I can repay that. I am not daft. I realise that if you don't win games then you won't receive that kind of support. Time is something that managers just don't get. I certainly don't want five or six years to get it right.'

By January, O'Neill's Villa were producing some impressive wins on the road but dropping points at home. The transfer window has been criticised by many managers for causing a mad scramble, inflating prices and unsettling players. O'Neill is no different. 'It's a crazy idea,' he told the *Daily Mail*. 'I don't understand the logic behind it. I thought our transfer system in the first place was half-decent. Then along comes young Bosman [a

Belgian player who challenged the rules of football transfers], who was quite right to pursue his case, and it has all changed. I have spoken to other managers about it but no one I know likes the system. It is condensed into January; everyone is scurrying around. It's frenetic, the amount of work you think you can do – you could be chasing around like a scalded cat for weeks and still not have made any headway. That is why it is so difficult for managers – we are all chasing the same players. And how many clubs do their main shopping in January? Summer would be better for all deals.'

Speaking of Lerner, he continued: 'I know he will want to do things if at all possible. I know he will be very supportive. Of course, we will not be the only club trying to strengthen. I know he really wants to improve the club; he is no fool, he wants to do something. He will be depending on me to make him aware of what is necessary. He has seen quite a few games now and he will support me. That is all I can ask of him. People have been asking me for ages what we will be doing. I can give no guarantees, but it won't be for the want of trying.'

An intriguing FA Cup third-round tie pitted O'Neill's Villa against Manchester United at Old Trafford. Sir Alex Ferguson had orchestrated the short-term signing of O'Neill's old Celtic hero Henrik Larsson in order to keep his squad fresh in the early stages of 2007. Having Henrik Larsson as an opponent was not something the Ulsterman relished. Ahead of the tie he talked about how he tried to sign the Swede for Aston Villa: 'I talked about him some time back, but his family were settled in Sweden and I asked the question at the time and he was pretty well settled. When I met him, when he was inducted into the Scottish Hall of Fame, I didn't even pose the question. I would not have expected him to be phoning me up saying, "I am heading to Manchester United, do you mind." He owes me absolutely nothing and I am hoping that is reciprocated. It is not a problem and I wish him all the best and he will do wonderfully well. I am not wistful, other than being delighted for him. Those days with Henrik at Celtic have passed and if it was only for a couple of months, it is not eventually where I want Aston Villa to go. It does not mean I would not want some experienced players around me, but I don't really want to ruin a decent relationship that I had with him. He might have arrived here and maybe found life was not so rosy and maybe I didn't pick him in games, so I really don't want a Henrik Larsson knocking on my door every single day saying, "I should have started the games," especially if we have got people who are capable of keeping him out of the team. He has been and still is a quality player. He went to Barcelona and his only gripe was he did not play regularly enough, but you are talking about great players like Ronaldinho and Samuel Eto'o keeping him out of the team. When he got into the side, he scored goals. With the number of games United are going to be involved in, then Sir Alex needs something else.'

It seemed inevitable that Larsson would be in the thick of the action at Old Trafford, and he opened the scoring ten minutes after the restart with a smart finish that highlighted the predatory skills O'Neill had valued so much. Despite a Milan Baros equaliser, another United super-sub, Ole Gunnar Solskjaer, hit a last-minute winner to dump O'Neill's side out of the competition at the first hurdle. 'Henrik Larsson scored the goal and he is always capable of doing that,' a disappointed O'Neill said after the game. 'People used to ask me if he could only score goals in Scotland but, as far as I am concerned, he can score goals in any league of his choice. I never thought for one minute he could not score in the Premiership. He has gone on to prove that.'

Aston Villa's league season, as it had done so often in recent years, tailed off without the draw of cup competition and 2006/07 they finished eleventh in the league. Their campaign was hampered by too many draws, though O'Neill had organised a team that was difficult to beat. 'I am satisfied with the way we have ended the season and our football has been pleasing as well,' he told *The Sun.* 'It won't make a jot of difference when the new season kicks off, but there has been a confidence about our play recently. I know the expectations will be higher next season, but there is a good feeling about this side. Maybe some people got carried away with the start of the season we had.'

He continued in the *Birmingham Post*: 'It really was our mid-season that was a disappointment to us, but I do feel there is now a good feel about this side. I feel we have a bit of pace, a bit of enthusiasm, a bit of energy and a bit of ability. We have not lost that many games – only three teams, I believe, have lost more than us, but we have drawn too many.'

'I didn't miss football,' he told the *Mirror*. 'I didn't miss any of it because I did not have the time or the inclination to miss any of it. But as things started to improve at home, I wanted to get back into it. I would not have taken the break willingly. I would have stayed in the game until I felt the game no longer wanted me or results were so poor that I had to go. It was not a relief for me to leave the game. I don't like talking about it. Because I am a cynical person myself, I feel there is always a view that some people might think I am hiding behind something. I also know that everybody in this life has problems. Of course, there is a perspective you put things into, but you are not unique in being able to do that. As far as my wife's health is concerned, who knows what is round the corner. Your life changes, no doubt, but everyone on this earth has personal concerns. I don't have a monopoly on that. And it should not blunt your enthusiasm or your determination. I see things in a different perspective, but often people seek to use seeing things in a broader perspective as a euphemism for losing your intensity. That has not happened to me. My intensity is very much still there. In fact, I don't think I have really changed as a person that much in the last thirty years. All the ambitions I had as a player and all the determination I had and was known for are still there. That is in my make-up. I came back into the game mainly because of my wife's improving health. At Aston Villa, an opportunity arose and I did not want that to pass. If ever there was a place to go into and try to restore former glories, it was Aston Villa.'

With a full summer to mould his own squad, O'Neill

wasted little time in securing the services of England Under-21 captain Nigel Reo-Coker from West Ham United. Gone were flops such as Juan Pablo Angel, Aaron Hughes and Gavin McCann and in their place came fast, powerful and technically adept players such as Ashley Young, John Carew and Stilian Petrov. All had shown their quality at the highest level and were acquired on a reasonable budget. While billionaire owner Randy Lerner supported his forays into the transfer market, O'Neill was aware he would not be able to compete with the Premier League's biggest clubs who were spending huge sums of money. The Lerner/O'Neill approach was a sensible one based on young players, mainly from the home nations. 'Randy Lerner wants to bring the good days back to Villa,' he told the *Mirror*. 'The new training ground, for instance, is magnificent. He doesn't expect overnight success and he doesn't expect to be challenging for stuff until there is an infrastructure in place. He wants to build a football club here. I think he has a trust in me and I want to repay that. I have a driving ambition to make the football club successful. When I had my year away, I was aware there is only so much time people will allow you to stay out of the game. When you come back, you come back to win football matches.'

'The last thing I am going to do is end up bankrupting a football club,' he told the *Independent*. 'In this day and age you have to be very careful because things are escalating at such a rate. Trying to find value for money is exceptionally difficult, but if all those things are there, we will try to do it. I have dismissed absolutely nothing, but I

am going to try and build a squad capable of competing –
not someone who might come in for two games and be an
"impact" signing and not really be value for money. You
see the escalation in process and someone who you
thought you would be able to get for X is now X plus Y.
Part of you questions it and part of you thinks "Do you go
along with it?" because other teams are strengthening their
sides. I am going to do that – the owner has given me the
responsibility, for want of a better word, to do it and this
is what I am looking at.'

However, while Chelsea, backed by Roman Abramovich,
and Manchester United – who had never been afraid to
spend big when necessary– had inflated the British
transfer market, competition for quality signings was at an
all-time high and improving on their eleventh-placed
finish in 2006/07 would be no easy matter.

By the start of the 2007/08 season O'Neill's side had
begun to take shape with a combination of devastating
pace and power that was sure to test even the most battle-
hardened Premier League rearguards. Ashley Young and
Gabriel Agbonlahor, two of the quickest players in the
division, were supported by the giant Norwegian John
Carew, who had earned his spurs with a series of eye-
catching performances for Valencia. The campaign began
with an inauspicious defeat to Liverpool before a goalless
draw with Newcastle at St James' Park. Villa's first win of
the campaign came at home to Fulham before a 5-0
drubbing of Wrexham in the League Cup.

The tie threw up one of those rare occasions that showed
just how long O'Neill had been in management. The trip

to Wrexham gave him the chance to square up against one of his former players, Brian Carey, who was a player at Leicester when O'Neill was boss. Having had a rocky relationship with one of his former managers in Brian Clough, O'Neill was now keen to give a glowing reference to one of his former charges. 'We had a group of centre halves and I think he had a couple of injuries, but he had a good knowledge of the game,' he told the *Liverpool Daily Post*. 'Did I think he would go into management? I always thought there was a possibility he would do that. He had plenty of experience as a player. His general overview of football was worth listening to. He talked a lot of sense on football. It was a difficult stage because I was trying to win some games at Leicester, which was proving difficult, and trying to get to know the players. I thought he had a better understanding than most at that time of what a manager might be feeling. Some of the questions he would pose during conversations suggested that. He had an insight into how a manager was feeling, trying to win games and being under pressure to do so. I always got the impression with Brian, even though he was quite quiet, that he had the ability to go and manage because he was interested in that aspect. I realised he was on the same wavelength as I tried to build a team.'

With Villa finding their form in front of goal there was never a better time to face Jose Mourinho's Chelsea. Second-half goals from Zat Knight and Gabriel Agbonlahor earned an impressive 2-0 win over the former champions – forcing the rest of the league to sit up and take notice. The victory was no mean feat considering the powerful side Mourinho had built – fuelled by Abramovich's seemingly limitless war chest. The Russian oligarch left just seconds after Agbonlahor sealed the points, a fact not lost on Chelsea's enigmatic boss who chose to play down the incident. O'Neill, meanwhile, was adamant the result would bolster his players' belief that they could go out and compete with the league's Big Four. But, as so often happens in football, they failed to maintain momentum and lost by a single goal to Manchester City in their next league encounter. Such was the class of the Premier League, and the millions invested by clubs vying for a European place, that there really was no such thing as an easy game. A 2-0 win over David Moyes' Everton, another side hoping to sneak into a Champions League place, sent Villa into their League Cup tie with Leicester City in high spirits. Leicester had enjoyed great success in the competition under O'Neill, which, unfortunately for the Ulsterman, continued at Villa Park as Matt Fryatt's second-half goal sent the home side crashing out of the competition. Adopting the same smash and grab tactics employed under O'Neill, Leicester stunned an under-strength Villa side with the Ulsterman accepting blame for the defeat lay on his shoulders alone.

An incredible 4-4 draw with Tottenham saw October begin at a blistering pace but it was to be another inconsistent month for O'Neill's Villa. A home drubbing by Manchester United followed victory over West Ham before a disappointing draw at Bolton. Consistency was proving hard to come by for Villa but that was all about to change. Four league games in November bought four wins, with only one goal conceded and a derby victory over Birmingham City to boot. It was without doubt Villa's best spell under O'Neill and saw them climb the table significantly. But any good work during the last four weeks was completely undone at the start of December as Arsenal and Portsmouth took maximum points from their trips to Villa Park before draws with Sunderland and Manchester City. A Boxing Day clash with Chelsea produced another rousing encounter, which ended with three sendings off, two penalties and eight goals shared equally between the two sides. Wigan and Spurs were promptly dispatched as Villa entered 2008 intent on securing a European place, but success in knockout competitions continued to elude Martin O'Neill. Perhaps continuingly being drawn against Manchester United in the FA Cup did not help matters, with Rooney and Ronaldo netting the goals to dump Villa out in the third round.

With nothing but the league now to focus on, supporters were adamant their season would not fade out – a common feature over the previous five years. It was a lacklustre game and O'Neill felt his side did enough to earn a replay, but in the last five years of the FA Cup, Villa had met Manchester United three times at the third-round stage, severely hampering the club's progress. Under the watchful eye of England manager Fabio Capello, O'Neill rejected claims his young side had tried too hard to impress the new national boss, but there was no doubt Ashley Young and Gabriel Agbonlahor were attracting interest. O'Neill wanted to build his team around the two young stars and told the *Birmingham Post*: 'I wouldn't sell them. Gabby has been linked with Arsenal but they didn't make a bid and I am sure that some journalist wakes up in the morning and thinks "I'll just disturb a few people today" with a story like that. These two players have been a major reason why we have been doing so well this season and we wouldn't want to disturb it now. If Villa do not do anything in the next couple of seasons, then I am sure all bets are off and everything changes, but we are trying to do something here and they are the sort of players we want to build things around for the next six or seven years. Are they unbuyable? Yes – they will be going nowhere.'

But it was not just in attack that Villa were proving a threat. In Danish defender Martin Laursen O'Neill had unearthed a giant who brought security alongside the Swede Olof Mellberg. O'Neill bought players to fill very specific jobs in the Aston Villa side and they had begun to play a brand of football he found acceptable. Laursen had given them a solid foundation at the back and the pace of Villa's flair players made them a dangerous proposition on the counter attack. A 2-2 draw with Liverpool at Anfield underlined Villa's credentials as top four candidates but after taking just one point from Blackburn and Fulham, it was proving difficult for O'Neill to string a run of wins together. When on form, Villa were devastating and proved this once again with a 4-1 demolition of Newcastle before an edgy win at Reading. A visit to north London, where Arsenal are able to play their expansive passing game on the wide north Emirates pitch, is an intimidating one but Villa enjoy the challenge, and were unlucky not to leave with all three points after Niklas Bendtner's last-gasp equaliser. Indeed it was fortunate Villa had amassed so many points before the spring period as a dour winless streak in March saw defeats to Portsmouth, Sunderland and Manchester United.

By March, the top four had begun to break away from the chasing back meaning a place in Europe was the most realistic prize for Aston Villa and it proved the perfect motivation for the season's final stretch. Ten goals in two league games put Bolton and Derby to the sword before a stunning 5-1 drubbing of city rivals Birmingham at Villa Park. There has rarely been a more fruitful spell in front of goal for the Villains. The win against Birmingham was Villa's last of the campaign as they managed just two points from their last three games – but sixth place, up from eleventh the year before – was ample reward for a season of hard graft.

But the summer of 2008 was dominated by Gareth Barry's move to Liverpool, with the long-time player falling out with the club's hierarchy, who were desperate to keep him at Villa Park. O'Neill and Liverpool manager Rafael Benitez – never afraid to get involved with mud-slinging via the media – fell out over the Anfield club's public courting of his captain. For his part, Barry made little secret of his desire to move to Liverpool, with the lure of Champions League football too good to resist for a player who had spent the vast majority of his career in the Midlands. O'Neill remained hopeful his Villa project could tempt Barry to stay but Liverpool were readying a big money deal – and the England international would have to have the final say. Barry, in the end, opted to stay in the Midlands for one more season to see where O'Neill could take the club. But his failure to commit his future instantly did not endear him to the Villa Park faithful and he was given a rough ride by supporters.

One factor that had persuaded Barry to stay on was European football and this came in the form of an Intertoto Cup tie early in the summer. Drawn against Danish club Odense in the Intertoto Cup, a less than convincing Aston Villa side scraped through 3-2 on aggregate over the two games. O'Neill had walked the European route many times in his career, with varying degrees of success at Leicester City and Celtic, but now it was time to see how his Aston Villa side would cope with the rigours of UEFA Cup football. At Celtic, O'Neill was acutely aware of the need to guarantee European football past Christmas. While he was aware European competition would be a drain on his squad, it was necessary to attract better players to the club. Victory over the Danish minnows presented O'Neill's Villa a chance to earn their place in the UEFA Cup proper. In their way stood FH Hafnarfjordur, an Icelandic side who had earned recognition for beating Dunfermline in the 2004/05 season. A 4-1 win in Iceland meant it was job done for Villa, but a 1-1 draw at Villa Park in the return leg did little to excite the supporters. It had been an entertaining start to the 2008/09 season for Villa, who had beaten Manchester City 4-2 on the opening day of the season before losing 3-2 to Stoke the week after.

While Villa were bankrolled by an American billionaire,

the club was run on a tight budget, sensibly so, and O'Neill had proved a master player of the transfer market, bringing in quality players on a budget. James Milner, Newcastle's promising young midfielder, had already had a spell at Villa Park on loan but O'Neill swooped to sign him on a permanent basis in the summer. Milner certainly fit the bill for a typical O'Neill signing; English, versatile, technically brilliant and with an eye for goal; a future international in the making. 'James came in here with a big fee but he was not affected,' O'Neill commented. 'He knew the scene before he come to Villa from his loan season although the revamped training ground would have been new to him. He settled in very quickly and I am sure James would be the first one to say "you paid it, not me". But to me anyway he justified the fee. Players can crumble under transfer fees in certain places.'

But any future forays into the transfer market were about to become a great deal harder. With the summer transfer window preparing to slam shut, Manchester City were acquired by Sheikh Mansour bin Zayed al-Nahyan, bringing seemingly limitless funds to swell the Eastlands coffers. To mark their swift acquisition of Manchester City, the club's new administration paraded Brazilian playmaker Robinho as their star signing in a sensational £32 million swoop – breaking the British transfer record without breaking sweat. Events at Eastlands would soon distort the transfer market and in turn increase the value of footballers – ensuring value for money was hard to come by.

In order to secure a place in the group stages of the

UEFA Cup Villa would need to overcome Litex, of Bulgaria, and again O'Neill's side relied on their away form to get the job done, and managed just a draw on home soil. This worrying trend would need to be reversed if Villa were to compete with the competitions' stronger sides, but O'Neill was pleased to be through to the group stages. He commented: 'We have got some European evenings at Villa Park, which I am really looking forward to. I can't say I have talked to loads and loads of fans, but it is something they are definitely looking forward to. Does it show Aston Villa are back? If I stop to think about it, that is right. Everyone has to fight for it, but it is a step in the right direction for the football club. We are into the proper stages, the group stages. The advantages by a million miles outweigh any disadvantage you have. We have got a chance now for younger players to experience this.'

Drawn against Ajax, Hamburg, Slavia Prague and Zilinia, it was a tough group that would provide a varied challenge for Villa's relatively inexperienced European squad. As the season moved towards October, Villa were once again going strong, beating Sunderland and West Brom but defeats to Chelsea and Spurs kept them outside the top four.

The early stages of the 2008/09 season were all about European competition at Villa Park and O'Neill could not hide his delight at the calibre of teams coming to the Midlands. The prospect of facing Ajax, former European Champions was 'mouth-watering' and O'Neill was happy to be a part of the occasion. He told the *Birmingham Post*: 'Villa Park could be rocking against Ajax in the opening game. It is a step up in quality. If you look at some of the teams involved, for example AC Milan, Seville and Ajax, these are the sides with a real pedigree. I have said before being in this competition and making it through to the groups stages guarantees us some great European nights up until Christmas.' O'Neill believed ten teams in the competition could do well by plying their trade in the Champions League and it was up to the players to earn their place among the European elite. Ajax travelled to Villa Park in late October and it was the home side who took the points in an end-to-end match typical of the best European nights. 'Ajax are a fine side,' he told the *Birmingham Post*. 'They have got some very good players and are a fine passing team but in the midst of all this I cannot forget we too have some excellent players in terms of ability and the heart and desire which we showed tonight. I was told the atmosphere would be excellent and it was.'

If there was any worry that midweek football would hamper the team's domestic duties, there was little evidence following the Ajax tie as Wigan, Blackburn and Newcastle all tasted defeat at the hands of a buoyant Villa. O'Neill took his side to the Czech Republic for their clash with Slavia Prague in a hostile environment that had tested many of the European elite. Despite being forced to blood reserve keeper Brad Guzan, Villa were able to keep a clean sheet and stole the points through a solitary John Carew goal. Impressive home and away victories marked a dream start for the quickly-maturing Villa. It was surprising then, that Villa tasted defeat at home to Zilina, on paper the easiest game in their group before losing 3-1 to Hamburg. But Villa had done enough, they were through to the knockout stages and would compete in European football beyond Christmas, O'Neill's benchmark when at Celtic. Back home in the Premier League, November proved a difficult month for Villa. Successive defeats to Newcastle and Middlesbrough were followed by an impressive unbeaten streak seeing them through to 2009. A stunning 2-0 win against Arsenal at the Emirates and goalless draw with Manchester United delighted O'Neill, with each member of his small squad doing their bit to ensure the club could compete on multiple fronts. Everton, Bolton, West Ham and Hull were all beaten in December as Villa entered 2009 in a rich vein of form. Gareth Barry, by now forgiven by the Villa fans, was once again the heartbeat of the side but it was the frightening pace of Young and Agbonlahor that continued to delight supporters and pundits alike. Villa were a side capable of upsetting the Premier League's big guns and only needed consistency to challenge the top four.

Fortunately for the club, the third-round draw for the FA Cup saw them avoid Manchester United and travel to Priestfield for a clash with Gillingham, which they won with an unconvincing performance. In the Premier League they continued to pick up results with a resilience that delighted the manager. While a replay was needed to see off lowly Doncaster, progress was finally being made in the FA Cup. February saw the return of UEFA Cup football. With just 32 teams left in the competition Villa were drawn against an improving CSKA Moscow side, who had Champions League experience and boasted Yuri Zhirkov, Wagner Love and Russian international keeper Igor Akinfeev among their talented side. The Russians earned a 1-1 draw at Villa Park and O'Neill called for his side to do 'a men's job' and win in the Russian capital – still freezing in the long Russian winter. It proved too much for O'Neill's men, who crashed out of the competition in February. He told the *Mirror*: 'This has been a good experience and I did not want to give it up. If we get the opportunity to play in Europe on a more regular basis, as this club should, then these types of experiences should hold the team in good stead.'

Such was the size of his squad, Villa were forced to field an almost reserve team. More than 200 Villa fans made the long, expensive trip to Moscow and O'Neill repaid them with an invitation to dinner for all those who flew. O'Neill knew, with European football over, the league would have to be his number one priority to ensure their adventures in 2008/09 were not a one-off. He told the *Express*: 'We are looking at progression. I have no question Randy has the same dream as me and every Villa fan. If you had told me that we could finish in the top four this season, but had to forsake the UEFA Cup – it is very obvious that is the route I would go down. Losing in Moscow gives more definition to the season and where we are placed. Now I know where we go. I hope the fans understand in the long run.'

Knowing what was needed to secure European football next term, and with bags of experience from their recent heroics, O'Neill set about masterminding another top six finish. Defeat in Moscow proved hard to take, however, and it would take some time for Villa to recover. Chelsea, Manchester City and Spurs all got the better of O'Neill's men before a devastating 5-0 loss to Liverpool. Indeed it was not until May that Villa won again, with John Carew's solitary goal seeing off the challenge of relegation-haunted Hull. A win on the last day of the season secured sixth place once again, but with a nine-point margin over seventh placed Fulham.

The close season would be one of frustration for O'Neill, however, as Gareth Barry opted for a cut-price move to Manchester City, swayed by the project proposed by the cash-rich Eastlands outfit, and completed a £12 million move. O'Neill responded by signing England international winger Stewart Downing from recently relegated Middlesbrough. It came as little surprise when Downing left the Riverside, with speculation lingering for well over a year, and he opted for a move to Villa Park. With Young, Milner and now Downing, the Aston Villa midfield – with an English core – was the envy of many clubs in the Premier League. The new signing, though, would not make his debut until November due to injury.

If Manchester City's signing of Robinho twelve months previously sent shockwaves, then their lavish spending in the summer of 2009 only served to cement their status as the new force in the Premier League. 'All they have got is 38 league games and the league Cup and FA Cup, which doesn't start until January,' O'Neill told the *Belfast Telegraph*. 'I would say now that the top four has become a genuine top five. It has surprised me. Manchester City have gone and got some players that three months ago I didn't think was possible.' O'Neill was aware that City, who splashed out upwards of £20 million on Joleon Lescott, made value for money hard to come by in the Premier League. 'You think, well, you got quite close last year and suddenly another club has just stepped over you immediately before you can go on,' he continued. 'It kind of punctures you.' But rather than remain downhearted, O'Neill admitted it left him excited to see what City could do in the division, much like Chelsea when they were bought by Abromovich five years before.

For O'Neill's Villa, City were just another threat in a league now full of contenders. Tottenham Hotspur, rejuvenated under Harry Redknapp, Everton, the only team to break into the elite group in recent memory, and Villa all held credible claims to snatch a Champions League spot. It was set to be a pivotal season. But for O'Neill, it began with a disappointment as Roberto Martinez's Wigan Athletic took the points on the opening day of the 2009/2010 season with a 2-0 win at Villa Park. Up next for O'Neill was their UEFA Cup qualifying round against Rapid Vienna, who had posed some problems for Manchester United in the Champions League a decade before. They were a combative side who knew how to negotiate a European tie. After failing to get an away goal in Vienna, and leaving with a 1-0 defeat, it was paramount that Villa did not concede in the return leg. Unfortunately, Rapid did get on the scoresheet and, although Villa won the match 2-1, they were knocked out on away goals. It was a bitter blow for O'Neill, who was desperate to see European football return to Villa Park after their strong showing last season. But it was not to be. 'We should have got through,' he said. 'We should have had the game out of site before they scored and it was unfortunate.'

Perhaps defeat was a blessing in disguise. With competition for fourth place stronger than ever, having just domestic competition to concentrate on could have worked in Villa's favour. It would appear O'Neill did not share this view. As he had said, the positives of UEFA Cup football far outweigh the negatives and European adventures are what attract the best players. 'In the cold light of day, it is not the end of the world what has happened' he accepted. There was an even bigger pay cheque on offer in the form of Champions League football. But while the pain of European exit was still raw, it is credit to the character of the Villa side that it did not destroy their start to the season. Liverpool, Birmingham, Portsmouth and a rapidly improving Fulham were all dispatched before the end of September. Martin O'Neill's side were the early pace setters in the race for fourth. A meeting between Villa and Manchester City in the Midlands on 5 October provided a fascinating meeting between two top four contenders. Perhaps it was no surprise when the match finished one apiece, with Craig Bellamy cancelling out Richard Dunne's early opener.

Villa welcomed Carlo Ancelotti's league leaders in the next league game and fell behind to an early Didier Drogba goal. Goals in either half from centre-back pairing Richard Dunne and James Collins swung the game Villa's way, and they hung on to inflict a first league defeat on the west London side. While O'Neill's Villa had become known for their devastating counter-attacking football, they were also becoming a threat from set pieces, aided by summer acquisition Richard Dunne, who was perhaps unfortunately part of the Manchester City cull. A 5-1 hammering of Bolton as the season moved into November underlined Villa's credentials. But they were also beginning to enjoy some success in the league cup, something that had eluded Martin O'Neill during his time in the Midlands. They moved into the fifth round of the competition after seeing off Sunderland on penalties – largely down to the heroics of reserve keeper Brad Guzan, afforded a rare starting berth in the competition. In December Villa saw off Portsmouth in the quarter-finals of the League Cup with a 4-2 win thanks to an English contingent of Emile Heskey, James Milner, Stewart Downing and Ashley Young. It is difficult to assess whether a lack of European football was keeping the squad fresh but by December Villa were unstoppable, picking up a famous win at Old Trafford in the process courtesy of Gabriel Agbonlahor's match winner.

A goalless draw with Arsenal in the league had Arsène Wenger infuriated, accusing Aston Villa of playing a long-ball game. O'Neill saw this as a grave insult. He fumed: 'If that is what he saw, that is a ridiculous statement. He has made a few ridiculous statements in his time here and that is as good as any. That's the only annoyance at the end of it all. Anybody who saw the game would take that viewpoint. Ashley Young didn't have time to play any long balls when he was taking that left-back to the cleaners. It's an appalling insult.' O'Neill is always the first to leap to the defence of his players, particularly with a cup final to prepare for. Villa are one of the most attractive sides in the Premier League with a boss who will fight to protect them.

At the start of 2010 O'Neill had another chance to return to the league cup final, with Blackburn Rovers standing in the way of a trip to Wembley. The first leg was comfortably controlled by the home side, who won 3-1. But the return fixture was a tense affair, with uncertain defending mixed with moments of inspiration in a ten-goal thriller. A two-goal salvo from Nikola Kalinic hauled Rovers back into the tie before Stephen Warnock, James Milner, Heskey, Agbonlahor and a Steven N'Zonzi own goal put Villa back in charge. Jonas Olsson and Brett Emerton netted as Villa nerves continued to show but Ashley Young's 90th minute goal ended the scoring, and sent Villa to Wembley with a 7-4 aggregate win. A rollercoaster ride was something the Villa fans could have done without, but O'Neill preached patience. 'These players are capable of fighting back,' he said. 'It is better if the crowd stay with them.' But he was delighted to have another shot at the League Cup, the chance to win his third and finally bring a trophy to the silverware-starved Villa Park faithful.

But in Villa's way stood Manchester United. A name synonymous with Wembley finals and used to winning more often than not. It was a tough task but Villa had won at Old Trafford already, and fancied their chances. A Wembley date had pundits purring at O'Neill's managerial talents and comparisons between his opposite number, Sir

Alex Ferguson, were rife. Could O'Neill be the man to take over once the Scot relinquishes control at Old Trafford? O'Neill claims it is the impossible job. 'I have never thought about it at all, not for one second,' he told the *News of the World*. 'Number one, I think Sir Alex will decide and I think in about the year 2033 when he decides, "Yeah I think the Champions League has just gone past me for the final time", and then I'll have departed the earth long before him. I really enjoy my job here and trying to win a couple of competitions in the next couple of seasons is what it is all about.'

But there are certain similarities between the two. Ferguson's dominance in the 1990's was based around an English nucleus, something O'Neill has unashamedly employed at Villa. In an age of foreign imports, it is a refreshing sight. 'I do feel the heartbeat of the football club should be fundamentally English,' he continued. 'It doesn't mean I hold every single principle by it, but the heartbeat should be the league in which you are playing.'

The Wembley final was unusually open for a cup showpiece. In an explosive start United defender Nemanja Vidi? was caught out by the pace of Agbonlahor and brought the striker down. James Milner scored the resulting penalty but the Serb stayed on the pitch, without so much as a card, a decision that baffled O'Neill. With their full complement of players, United were able to turn the match around thanks largely to the inspirational Wayne Rooney. Feeling Villa were robbed, O'Neill said: 'I think it was plain for all to see. It's an inexplicable decision and I don't really understand it. It was a goal-scoring opportunity and the player is fouled in the area. It is straightforward from an otherwise fine referee.'

Defeat was hard to take for O'Neill, particularly in an unjust manner, as he clearly felt. He was proud of his young charges, who are continuing to learn on both a domestic and international stage. There is no doubt that the O'Neill formula has worked wonders at Aston Villa and there is genuine belief that a place in the Champions League is within their grasp. While the disappointment of the defeat will linger, O'Neill had taken Aston Villa to Wembley, their first under Randy Lerner, and there is sweeping optimism at Villa Park. The supporters have the scent of silverware in their nostrils, and crave more. Martin O'Neill has made the side a formidable force in knockout competitions, and one of the genuine contenders for a top four place. Under O'Neill, the only way is up.